T0196944

I AM

REVEALED

I AM
REVEALED

KNOWING GOD ON A FIRST-NAME BASIS

MIKE BAKER

I AM REVEALED
KNOWING GOD ON A FIRST-NAME BASIS

Cover Design: Anissa Ortiz, Eastview Christian Church

iUniverse books may be ordered through booksellers or by contacting:

iUniverse
1663 Liberty Drive
Bloomington, IN 47403
www.iuniverse.com
1-800-Authors (1-800-288-4677)

ISBN: 978-1-5320-5393-1 (sc)
ISBN: 978-1-5320-5394-8 (e)

Library of Congress Control Number: 2018908100

Print information available on the last page.

iUniverse rev. date: 09/13/2018

DEDICATION PAGE

To Sara, Mikey, Caleb, Monica and Jessica – my favorite people – in whose company I have learned the most about God.

CONTENTS

ACKNOWLEDGEMENTS

There are times when I thought I would never get this book done. No really, I thought it wasn't going to happen. But the following people made it possible through their prayers, encouragement, and input:

My wife, Sara, who put up with my deadlines and the accompanying stress and moods.

My leadership team, who inspire me and make me want to be a better lead.

The staff at Eastview Christian Church – I'm surrounded by greatness.

The elders at Eastview Christian Church – I am humbled to serve with men who are truly interested in shepherding the flock God has entrusted to us.

The people of Eastview Christian Church – may God continue this incredible love affair between us for many years to come.

INTRODUCTION

My brother-in-law's name is Rei. And Rei is the name I use to address him (aside from the occasional times I call him Hermano). But there is more to him than just this name. Rei is from the capital city of El Salvador, San Salvador; and like most people from Hispanic cultures, Rei has an official name that's much longer than the one I call him. His full name is Jose Reinaldo Gonzales Jimenez. Each of these names reveals something significant about him.

In his home country, Rei would be called Jose Reinaldo because his first name (Jose) is so common. So the Reinaldo part of his name (the part we shorten to Rei) signifies exactly which Jose he is. Rei's third name, Gonzalez, is the surname of his father's side of the family. The fourth name, Jimenez, reveals his mother's family heritage.

To me he is known simply as Rei, but there is significance in that name. When I hear his name, I think *brother-in-law* and, therefore, connect his name with being part of my family. I know Rei as a hardworking brick mason who often travels with his job. Like me, Rei is a soccer fan and an even bigger fan of a great meal. He smiles easily. When I say his name, I'm reminded of all those things. When I hear the name Rei, all my experiences with him come instantly to mind. His name has meaning for me because I know the man behind the name.

But there is still more to who Rei is ---- things I don't know about him, which are revealed in his other names. This is true with all of our relationships. Though we know most people on a first-name basis, a person's middle name, maiden name, family name, and even nickname can reveal so much more. The more we know about these other names, the more we know about the person.

The premise of this book is that this is true of God as well. If God has a "first name," I guess it would be . . . well, God. We know God as a supreme being of the universe. The name of God carries great weight. The very mention of his name evokes ideas about supremacy, power, totality, and control. Though some use his name irreverently at times, it still retains its place above all other names and titles. Think about it: What other name signifies something higher than the name God? Certain mythologies, religions, and worldviews may have lowercase "gods," but there is only one God with a capital *G*.

So when I call out to him, I usually call him by this name. I begin most of my prayers with "Dear God," I sing songs at church about God, and I speak to others of God --- but is there more about God to be discovered? Does he, like most of us, carry other names that help describe him more fully and reveal more of who he is?

I believe so. In fact, the word *God* is not the personal name he used in Scripture to introduce himself to his people. In the Scriptures, the God of Abraham, Isaac, and Jacob appeared to Moses in a burning bush on Mt. Sinai (Horeb). It was here, as recorded in the third chapter of Exodus, that God called Moses to return to Egypt and lead his people out of slavery and into the promised land. The conversation was quite extensive, but for our purposes we will focus only on one question Moses asked God. In essence he asked, "What is your name?" He surely reasoned that if he was going to worship God, represent God, and lead God's people, then he should know God by name. Besides, he anticipated that the people would ask about it.

So God introduced himself as I AM, saying, "I AM WHO I AM. This is what you are to say to the Israelites: 'I AM has sent me to you'" (Exodus 3:14). The footnote in my NIV says that this word could also be translated *I WILL BE WHAT I WILL BE.* Either way, I AM doesn't seem like that great a name until you consider what it signifies. The Hebrew word *hayah,* which is translated *I AM* in the English, means "To be or exist."[1] When God introduced himself to Moses, he gave this mysterious name that seems to indicate the very essence of living or being. The God of Mt. Sinai had given Moses a name to call him that indicated his greatness and power at the supreme level. God had revealed himself as the one who holds all life together. It is with the knowledge of this name and its meaning that Moses finally had the courage to obey God's call to lead.

Still, Moses must have been a bit mystified, so it should not surprise us that the name remains mysterious to us all these years later. Perhaps because of our limited perspective and because of the name's immensity, the full meaning is lost on us. Imagine this conversation with God:

"What is your name?"

"Being."

"You mean, like, your actual being alive, or all being in general?"

"Yes."

"Well, where did you come from?"

"I exist."

"Yeah, I know you are here now, but what is your starting point?"

"I AM."

It is humanly impossible to fully know God --- to fully understand and comprehend the great I AM. But Moses discovered more about God later on the mountain, and the Bible gives us some more glimpses. God reveals himself through many Old Testament names and titles that describe his attributes and give insight into his person. As his great power intersects the lives of the human world that he created, we humans learn about him and his other names that reveal more of his greatness.

God most completely revealed himself to us by sending his Son, Jesus, to walk among us. In time and space, God became a man. We know that Jesus is God revealed because the Bible plainly teaches it to be so. Jesus also confirmed this in his ministry on the earth. The very name God had revealed to Moses in Exodus 3 is a name Jesus used to describe himself. When he was being questioned about his authority, Jesus stated emphatically, "Very truly I tell you, . . . before Abraham was born, I am!" (John 8:58). Verse 59 shows us that Jesus' critics who were hearing this knew exactly that he was stating his divine nature.

God introduced himself as I AM in his encounter with Moses on the mountain, and he has been giving us insight into that name ever since. Through creating, providing for, healing, watching over, protecting, guiding, saving, and being king of his people, God has demonstrated who he is. We are embarking on a study of some of the names and descriptions of God that reveal his character and person. I am glad you have decided to join me on this journey. As we delve into the God stories and study these names, my prayer is that you will deepen your walk with him and his Son, Jesus, by faith. It is in these very names that God is revealing to us who he was – and is. And what difference that should make in our lives today!

I AM is for us.

I AM is with us.

I AM is revealed to us.

GOD
Elohim El.o.*heem*

The word *Elohim* is the plural form of *el,* a common word for
any god. Most of the time when the plural title Elohim "is
used for the true God it has singular masculine verbs."[2]

ONE

CREATOR
{GENESIS 1:1-31}

J.I. PACKER

---

*How may we form a right idea of God's greatness? The Bible teaches us two
steps that we must take. The first is to remove from our thoughts of God limits
that would make Him small. The second is to compare Him with powers and
forces which we regard as great.*

A couple of months before I was scheduled to speak in a southeast
Texas town, the guy who was organizing the weekend called me.
After spending some time with the typical small talk, discussing
travel details and the upcoming event, he paused.

"Mike," he said, "I need to ask a huge favor of you for this weekend." Not knowing exactly what his request might be, I assured him I'd do whatever he needed.

"For the time you're here with us, I need you to go by another name."

"OK. . ." I replied cautiously, "What's the deal?"

He went on to explain that a former pastor of his church (the church hosting the area-wide event) had been dismissed in a negative fashion; and that person, unfortunately, shared my name. There was simply no way my friend could advertise the event with a name that conjured up so much emotional pain. I didn't really know how to respond, so I agreed. We decided on using my middle name, Robert, for the weekend.

When I arrived, the hotel reservation was under this "assumed name." The posters plastered on the walls all over the church building had my real photo, but not my real name. My friend used my middle name to introduce me to youth group kids, sponsors, and church members. For three days, I preached to these people, ate with these people, chatted with them, and prayed with them; but it's hard for me to say they got to know me. In all my ministry experiences, I have never left a group of people with a more disconnected feeling. Because no one called me Mike all weekend, it was like it never happened. I made up my mind on the plane ride home --- never again!

We really can't get to know someone until we know him by name. A person's name becomes attached to his personality and in some ways describes who that person truly is. The totality of who one is can be expressed simply by saying his name. It's the same way with God. Maybe this is why Genesis introduces him by name in the very first sentence of the Bible.

We really can't get to know someone until we know him by name.

IN THE BEGINNING

Our discovery of God begins in the only place it logically can: in the beginning of human history as recorded in the Bible. With three simple Hebrew words --- that are translated into English as "In the beginning God created" --- we are introduced to the absolute supreme being of the universe with a time (*hereshith*, translated "in the beginning"); an action (*bara,* translated "created");[3] and finally a name, which we will get to shortly. Though these words are simple, they are powerfully descriptive concerning the greatness of the name of God, as we will discover together in this chapter.

"In the beginning" actually reveals a human limitation to knowing God, a limitation that magnifies his greatness while simultaneously hindering our complete discovery of him. So, before we are introduced for the first time to God by name, let us address this issue. Our limitation is that we can only understand God within the confines of human history that he began with a word. Before that explosive, eternal moment when God said, "Let there be light," everything was literally in the dark. We remain "in the dark" in our understanding, to some extent. The apostle Paul expressed the futility of our trying to understand God completely. He wrote, "Oh, the depth of the riches of the wisdom and knowledge of God! How unsearchable his judgments, and his paths beyond tracing out!" (Romans 11:33).

In getting to know God, we must acknowledge that there is an entire history of God in eternity past that we have been given no direct information about. God was here before the world was ever set spinning on its axis, before time had ever been measured in minutes and hours, way before the sun had ever risen, and before anyone was around to observe his greatness. "Before the mountains were born or you brought forth the whole world, from everlasting to everlasting you are God" (Psalm 90:2).

3

AN APPROPRIATE NAME

So what name can possibly be given to describe this bigger-than-anything-we-know God? What do you call one who was around before our historical time line? Well, the first name given for God in the opening line of Genesis is a name that points to his greatness. The name is Elohim. The simple translation is *God*, but there is much more to it than that.

Fast-forward many years, from Genesis through the Israelites' deliverance out of Egypt and the crossing of the Red Sea, and then beyond their forty years in the wilderness. When the people of God finally settled in the land of their inheritance, there was no shortage of gods among the conquered Canaanite people. The people of the land worshipped many gods (see Deuteronomy 4:28; 6:14, for example). Here are a few by name:

- a god who went by the name Baal (Numbers 25:3)
- a god named Ashtoreth (Judges 2:13)
- a god whose name was Chemosh (2 Kings 23:13)
- a god called Molek (Leviticus 20:2)

The generic word used for any god was simply *el*. This one word was used in reference to the gods of Canaan, but it was not adequate as a name for the God worshipped by the land's new inhabitants. Israel's one true God was superior to all other gods. The word *el* just wouldn't do. The plural form, Elohim, is the proper name Moses used when he was led by the Spirit to detail the history of God and his people.

Some scholars believe the plural usage of this Hebrew word referenced the reality of the Trinity, and others think that this was simply a way of indicating God's majesty. Both, of course, are true. What we discover in the first verse of the Bible is a name for God that indicates his plurality of personalities. He has superiority, majesty, and power. He has preexistence over every other being in the universe. Bruce Waltke states it this way: "this name of God represents his transcendent relationship to creation. He is the quintessential expression of a heavenly being. God, unlike human beings, is without beginning, begetting, opposition, or limitations of power."[4] He is the God of gods.

THE GOD BEHIND THE NAME

Now that we have been introduced to Elohim, we can dig deeper into the personality of God and our discovery of him as Creator. Because there is a beginning to human history --- and since God was there when it started --- it follows that there was a time when there was no creation but there was a creator God. As we consider Elohim's preexistent state, there are at least two surface discoveries that give insight into this great God who is not bound by time. These two clues will help us acknowledge that he is bigger than all creation.

Discovery #1: God was fine without us

God didn't *need* to make the world. The creation he would eventually bring into existence was not something he had to have to make his own existence meaningful. He was here long before mint chocolate chip ice cream (though I can't comprehend the nonexistence of *that!*), roller coasters, and the laughter of children at play. We must understand (as much as is humanly possible) that before world time began, God was experiencing the joy, love, community, fellowship, and belonging of the Trinity.

Jesus prayed about this eternal past: "and now, Father, glorify me in your presence with the glory I had with you before the world began" (John 17:5). God was doing just fine without the creation. So why did he create the universe and everything in it? The answer is found in our second discovery about Elohim.

Discovery #2: It is in God's nature to create

To fully express his great power, splendor, compassion, and ability, God creates.

- The beauty found in creation reflects his nature.
- The power found in creation verifies his awesome presence.
- The detail found in creation indicates his complexity.
- The reproducing qualities found in created beings demonstrate his life-sustaining energy.

God's nature is to create because through his creation he is able to communicate, reveal, and display his greatness. And this is exactly how we can discover who Elohim is. From our earthbound, creation-observing perspective we may get only a glimpse of the supremacy of Elohim as Creator. But what we *can* see is quite impressive.

> **God's nature is to create because through his creation he is able to communicate, reveal, and display his greatness.**

Bara ("created") is a Hebrew word that indicates the making of something out of nothing. God didn't have some huge home-improvement store in the sky where he could buy Sequoia-size timber, billions of nails, and oceans of paint. God made everything you and I see, and he made it out of nothing. "What is seen was not made out of what was visible" (Hebrews 11:3).

The Hebrew word *bara* is not a verb used for the creative work of just anyone in the Bible. As R. Kent Hughes explains, "Moses uses very specialized and honed vocabulary here. 'Created' is only used of God in the Bible. Only God creates."[5] The greatness of God is incredibly expressed in his ability to create. And though our experience of God's greatness doesn't reach back before the world began, we can actually experience his greatness through observing what he created.

CREATION OBSERVED

We can gain insight into God by observing his creation, but God is not just great because he *can* create or because his creation is so awesome. We can deepen our understanding of him by recognizing the *way* in which he created the heavens and the earth. In the biblical account of creation, we read that God creates by his word, his work, and his breath.

Creation through his word

In the creation story we discover that God creates by his word. "And God said" is the three-word phrase that recurs six times, at the beginning of each day, in reference to God's creation (Genesis 1:3, 6, 9, 14, 20, 24; with a few "Then God saids" thrown in at verses 11, 26, 29). He spoke and amazing stuff happened. And I mean cosmic amazing, like an ocean was formed - not like you just won at Bingo. Every day of creation was marked with the incredible phrase "And God said," revealing the great generative power and authority of his voice as it echoed through the universe. As David declared, God's voice is as powerful as thunder (Psalm 18:13).

- By God's word, there was light on day one.
- By his word, there was the expanse of the sky and the heavens on day two.
- By his word, there was land and sea on day three. By his word, he also filled this land with every plant, tree, bush, shrub, vegetable, and fruit on day three.

- By his word, all the stars and planets in the farthest corners of our universe appeared--- sparkling or reflecting light --- on day four.
- By his word, every water creature and every soaring bird came into being on day five.
- By his word, every furry little creature, large lumbering ox, and fleet-footed gazelle filled the earth he had formed, on day six.

"By faith we understand that the universe was formed at God's command" (Hebrews 11:3).

At an early age, we each are surrounded with authoritative voices that command our action. Most children come to realize that their parents' words have weight. The word *no* is the final answer to questions like "Can my friend Spike spend the night?" and "Can I have another candy bar? I've only had six" and "Can I have thirty dollars to get a swastika tattoo with my friends?" On the other hand, a *yes* may allow children to participate in a sport they love or to take music lessons or to enjoy the latest video game.

Our parents' words have real power, the power to determine the course of our lives --- either negatively or positively.

As we grow into independence, hoping to be able to "do whatever I want," we learn that we never really outgrow this submission to the words of people in our lives. We still must respond to certain people whose words have authority. We answer to teachers in school, coaches in sports, police officers in society, judges in the courtroom, and bosses at work. We are subject to these people because their words are "the final word" for us. When they speak, we must listen.

God the Creator reveals from the very beginning that everything is subject to his word. His voice is absolute. When he talks, all creation is eternally directed. Every word that comes from his mouth moves everything you and I know and observe. When he speaks, the whole universe listens! How great is our

God that his word wields this kind of authority and power? Truly amazing! Our proper response is a humble, fearful awe --- and God desires this worship from us. The prophet Isaiah quoted God, saying, "These are the ones I look on with favor: those who are humble and contrite in spirit, and who tremble at my word" (Isaiah 66:2).

Creation by his work

I discovered in third grade art class that I wasn't very good at working with my hands. The assignment was to make something out of a block of clay. The teacher allowed our imaginations to soar as each student decided what to work on. I chose to make a panther paperweight. Please don't ask me why. What's important to know is that even with my two hands and all the sculpting tools in the world, I could not have constructed anything that came close to resembling the big cat I envisioned. I ended up making a clay dish that I think became a Father's Day gift for my dad. I wanted to create a cool sculpture, but the work of my hands simply didn't measure up.

There are some words in the first two chapters of Genesis that indicate that God worked with his hands as well --- only he had better results than I did! Beginning in Genesis 1:7, we find that as Creator, Elohim "made" things in the creation process. This word (not *bara* as in verse 1, but *asah*) denotes work done with the hands, since its meaning is "to do" or "to fashion."[6] The implication is that our God not only spoke the universe into existence; he also rolled up his sleeves, as it were, and put his hands to the task. We are not sure how all God's words joined with his work to accomplish the task. We simply understand that what you and I witness as creation was handmade by God.

Every word that comes from his mouth moves everything you and I know and observe.

9

A closer examination of Genesis 1, 2 indicates the literal handiwork of God

- He made the sky (1:7).
- He made the two great lights and the stars (1:16).
- He made the wild animals (1:25).
- He set out to make man in his image (1:26).
- He saw all that he had made (1:31).
- He made the earth and the heavens (2:4).
- He made trees (2:9).
- And finally, he made a woman from the rib of Adam.

Additionally, there are other hands-on words in our text, like "created" (1:21), "formed" (2:7), and "planted" (2:8). God worked with his mighty hands to accomplish his creation.

God's hands-on participation in the creation process reveals more about greatness. How big is this Elohim who with his hands can actually hold the sun and moon as if they were kickballs on the playground? How great are the fingers that flip stars without number into the vast regions of the universe, calling them by name? (see Psalm 147:4). What size hands must one have to release blue whales into the depths of the ocean? And yet, how delicate a touch to take a single rib and form something as beautiful as a women. The fact that God created with his hands what is bigger than we can imagine places us in a very vulnerable and awestruck position. In pondering the creation, we discover that Elohim has an unfathomable size that literally overwhelms us.

Imagine how Job must have trembled as God described himself in a larger-than-life way in rebuttal to Job's complaints. God asked Job a series of questions like these:

- "Can you bring forth the constellations in their seasons?" (Job 38:32).
- "Do you send the lightning bolts on their way?" (v. 35).

- "Who can tip over the water jars of the heavens?" (v. 37).
- "Does the hawk take flight by your wisdom?" (39:26).

> **Imagine how Job must have trembled as God described himself in a larger-than-life way in rebuttal to Job's complaints.**

The obvious answer was, only Elohim can do those things --- because only he was big enough to create it all by hand in the first place. We, like Job, are left to sit silently in reverence of his work of creation.

Creation by his breath

If you aren't completely overwhelmed by the greatness of God at this point, I'm not sure there's much more I can do to impress you. But I'll try. There is yet another treasure behind the creation and the name Elohim that may be the greatest discovery of all. God did not just display his awesome power by speaking from a distance in his eternally booming voice. Nor did he limit his interaction with creation to putting his hand to the work and getting involved in the world's formation. By far, God's most powerful expression in creation came when he breathed life into man. God's gift of life's breath also animated other creatures, but his intent to make man in his image forever separated mankind from every other thing that God had made.

Most Bible teachers understand chapter 2 of Genesis as a kind of follow-up to the overview of creation described in the first chapter of the Bible. In his more detailed description, we discover some of the specifics of creation --- especially as they relate to the grand product of God's work, mankind. God declared that each phase of creation was "good." But it was only after he created man that God said, "*very* good" (Genesis 1:31, emphasis added). Elohim's creation by breathing pulled his whole creation project together and revealed still more of his character and greatness.

An understanding of a couple of Hebrew words gives us some details behind God's creation of humankind. The "Spirit" of God in Genesis 1:2 (*ruah* in Hebrew) is literally the breath, or wind, of God, "the creative Spirit of God."[7] We rightly understand it as the presence of the spirit in some insight that the Holy Spirit functions as the life-giving and creative breath of the Godhead. God spoke creation into being, and it was his breath, or Spirit, that moved to accomplish his word.

The word *neshamah*, translated *breath* in "breath of life" (Genesis 2:7), sometimes refers to everything that has breath (see 7:22). Sometimes having this breath equals being human (as in Joshua 11:11; Isaiah 2:22). And in Job 34:14 *neshamah* is the *breath* part of the phrase "spirit [*ruah*] and breath."[8]

So when we read Genesis 1:2 and then read 2:7 that God blew the "breath of life" directly into the nostrils of this handmade, dirt man, we get the sense that in some way the Spirit of God becomes the animating force of life in mankind.

Several years ago, the organization I worked for concluded that employees should be trained to respond to emergency situations that might arise in our ministry. We spent an entire day being certified by the Red Cross in CPR and emergency response. One part of our training included practicing mouth-to-mouth resuscitation on a dummy (no, not each other, just a realistic representation). Honestly, it felt a bit weird to place my lips on the mouth of a rubber human replica, but I did it to train. I distinctly remember thinking as I blew into this inanimate model that this must have been what it was like when God breathed into Adam (though my breath wouldn't be life-giving in the same way). I have never had the opportunity to breathe into a real person's mouth to keep him or her alive, but I can't think of many ways that would express more intimate sharing.

God's greatness in creation may be displayed best in his willingness to share his life-breath with Adam. We don't know exactly how God blew his breath into the man, but imagine the God of the universe gently holding this man, a wonderfully detailed yet lifeless lump of clay, in his hands. Somehow, God breathed into him, and he became living.

"Here the metaphor of shared 'breath' suggests a correspondence between Adam and his Maker that was expressed in Genesis 1:27 in the language of 'image.' This man of dust is in the image of God!"[9] In some way the wind of God that brought life to all creation through his Spirit now became the life-giving breath of man. It is a marvelous mystery and yet a wonderful truth. While only those who follow Jesus by faith are promised the indwelling presence of the Holy Spirit, there is something sacred and live-giving every time a human being inhales.

> **Imagine for a moment the God of the universe gently holding this man, a wonderfully detailed yet lifeless lump of clay, in his hands.**

NAMED BUT FORGOTTEN

God's first Bible name, Elohim, is the name God inspired Moses to write, by his Spirit, that most fully expressed his creative greatness. All the so-called gods of the Canaanites were not creators; they were *created*. In fact, those false gods found their origins in the hands of various human beings, each fashioning his god into what he wanted him to be. God's superiority is obvious. He is living, moving, powerful, and greater than any god by far. And the appropriate response of the people of God is to continue living in complete reverence and worship before their superior God.

But God's people in the Old Testament didn't do that.

Unbelievably, the people of the one true God allowed themselves to become curious about and enticed by the more exotic religious practices they saw; they followed the ways of the pagan peoples around them in worshipping many obviously false gods. This brought about God's most wrath-filled jealousy for his great name. Understandably, he could not tolerate his people worshipping inanimate objects instead of him. As God pointed out over and over again through his prophets, it was detestable to him (see 1 Kings 14:22-24; Ezekiel 5:8-9). The prophet Isaiah even described God's mockery of those who had turned to idols made from wood: "no one stops to think, no one has the knowledge or understanding to say, 'Half of it I used for fuel; I even baked bread over its coals, I roasted meat and I ate. Shall I make a detestable thing from what is left? Shall I bow down to a block of wood?'" (Isaiah 4:19). In fact, the people of God did bow down to many "blocks of wood."

The people of God must have forgotten his name, Elohim, the name that indicated greatness, complexity, and creativity. Either they forgot his name or forgot all that it represented. IF they had remembered Elohim, they would have maintained relationship with him alone and not abandoned him for weaker imitations.

I often find myself judging those people who directly benefited from God's awesome creation. As I think all the way back to Adam and Eve, I feel disappointment in humankind's rebellion against God. Adam and Eve were literally formed by God's hands and were brought to life by his breath, but could not keep from listening to another voice and then idolizing the fruit. Is this how humans respond to the God above all gods?

Perhaps this is very human indeed.

- Today we are more likely to speak with many words of ignorance to our cyber friends than to pay attention to the Word of the Creator.
- We have a tendency to turn our backs on the one who holds us in his hands, in order to embrace what we can hold in *our* hands.

- We are inclined to forget the God whose life is eternal, to get all we can out of this temporary, quickly fading life on earth.
- Even as we breathe the life-giving air that comes from God, we pursue many other things we "can't live without."
- Instead of bowing before God in awe, we flippantly take Elohim for granted.

How can you and I ever respond properly to our great, eternal, creator God? There is only one proper response, and that is worship. But we are often much more like the Old Testament people of God than we would probably care to admit. Instead of living a life of fearless devotion to his greatness and mercy, we embrace the silly gods of this world that hold absolutely no power.

Millions in our world today still bow down to images. Though Buddhist teachers might deny that they worship the image of Buddha, millions still flock to his many large images and have personal statues in their homes before which they pray. Hindus worship a variety of gods in many forms, including the chief gods Shiva and Vishnu. Many in our world literally bow down to "gods made by human hands," which "are no gods at all" (Acts 19:26).

Though most in America would not think of themselves as idol worshippers, it is unfortunately true that even sincere Christians can be deceived into placing their trust in the false idols of horoscopes, palm readings, transcendental meditation, and prosperity gospel teaching --- among other things.

Equally dangerous is the amount of time, energy, and money we pour into our material possessions. We live in a materialistic culture that lures us into adoration of the things we possess. But are the temporary silly gods of My Ginormous House, My Designer Clothes, or My Latest Gadget any more worthy of our devotion than the wooden idols were of the Old Testament Israelites' devotion?

Prayerfully, will you take a few moments to identify ways in which you are misplacing worship that only God deserves? And while we evaluate and eliminate the gods in our lives in order to worship Elohim, we can celebrate the redemptive work he continues to do by his grace in our lives.

CREATION CONTINUES

Graciously, our God Elohim didn't stop after the six days of his creation were complete. He rested to consecrate the seventh day, but his creative nature continued.

The role of Jesus

God created Adam in the beginning --- introducing human life into his created order --- but at just the right time, he created a way for us to spend eternity with him: he sent his Son, Jesus, into the world. Paul observed, "The first man was of the dust of the earth; the second man is of heaven" (1 Corinthians 15:47). This ties the creation of the world to the creation of an eternal people of God. When God observed the day in which he created mankind, he saw that 'it was very good' (Genesis 1:31), but when he commented on his Son, Jesus, he proclaimed, "With you I am well pleased" (Luke 3:22).

The creation of the world revealed the greatness of Elohim in his power to create life, but the sending of his Son created a way for eternal life for all who come to him by faith. Adam was a very good creation, but God was pleased with his Son's willingness to save all creation. Jesus was God's way of renewing his original, rebellious creation so that his people could worship him as he deserved. God is so creative that he gave his creations a chance to be re-created through Jesus. "Therefore, if anyone is in Christ, the new creation has come: The old has gone, the new is here!" (2 Corinthians 5:17).

Jesus was God's way of renewing his original, rebellious creation so that his people could worship him as he deserved.

Jesus is the Word, or the communication, of God that was spoken in the beginning. "In the beginning was the Word, and the Word was with God, and the Word was God" (John 1:1). And in the fullness of time he became flesh and blood to communicate God in an intimate way. Jesus became the human picture of "And God said." In the beginning, the voice of God thundered, "Let there be light" (Genesis 1:3), and it was glorious. But in Jesus we were able to see the glory of God. "The word became flesh and made his dwelling among us. We have seen his glory, the glory of the one and only Son, who came from the Father, full of grace and truth" (John 1:14).

The role of Scripture

God created eternal life through his Word Jesus, but he also creates through the written Word recorded for us in Scripture.

The Word of God was spoken through prophets and priests in the Old Testament and through prophets and apostles in the New Testament. These words come to us in the form of holy Scripture and *create* in us by cutting deep into our being and altering our hearts. The writer of Hebrews says, "The word of God is alive and active. Sharper than any double-edged sword, it penetrates even to dividing soul and spirit, joints and marrow; it judges the thoughts and attitudes of the heart" (Hebrews 4:12). God is creating a new person deep within as his Word gets to the core of who we are. God's living Word made us new creations, and his written Word continues to shape our hearts into his image.

The role of the Spirit

As from the beginning, God still creates by his Spirit. God was not content simply to behold his creation as an outside observer. He became involved with his creation by bringing it to life. In the same way, God did not simply create new life by coming close through Jesus. He continually creates life in us through his indwelling Spirit.

He created through his Spirit in the beginning, and he intended to create us into his people from the beginning. As the apostle Paul said, "We ought always to thank God for you, brothers and sisters loved by the Lord, because God chose you as first fruits to be saved through the sanctifying work of the Spirit and through belief in the truth" (2 Thessalonians 2:13).

A middle-aged man named Will recently returned to our church after an absence of nearly sixteen years. He had formerly been on staff here, but some sinful decisions on his part had led to his dismissal. In his discouraged state he chose a path away from God and lived a self-destructive existence of addiction, negativity, and bitterness. However, a providential word from a counselor challenged him to return to the place of his pain. He returned still hardened to God and the church, but we embraced him and prayed that God would move on his behalf.

Over a series of months, as the Word of God was preached, the Spirit moved, and the church welcomed him, a visible change in Will was apparent. This culminated in his own public rededication and the subsequent baptism of his teenage daughter on the same Sunday. The smile of joy on his face was visible evidence of a newly created heart!

Now he adds his presence, voice, and smile to our choir specials and serves with the love of Christ in our food pantry. Elohim's creation continues in him and in all of us who follow Elohim.

ELOHIM IS SUPERIOR TO ALL GODS

Elohim is superior to all gods because he is before all gods and before all creation. He is superior to all gods because though we, his creation, rebelled against his greatness, he created us anew by his living Word, Jesus. He is superior to all gods because he continually creates new hearts in disciples through his written Word and through the indwelling presence of his Spirit. By the creative wind of God, he sustains our lives. He is superior to all gods because only he could create what he has created, and only he could sustain it.

He returned still hardened to God and the church, but we embraced him and prayed that God would move on his behalf.

On the seventh day after God created the world, he rested. What must the eighth day have been like? The creation story doesn't give us details. Perhaps a brilliant red sun broke the dawn and stirred the man from his night's rest. The chirping of the birds filled his ears as he plucked a fresh pear from a tree and enjoyed its sweetness. The warm breeze felt silky on his skin, and he laughed as monkeys swung playfully from branch to branch. He ran to the river in the middle of the garden and stopped for a refreshing drink. All around him thousands of colors, sights, and sounds awaited discovery, each revealing a part of God's personality. The man breathed deeply the life-sustaining breath that God had blown into his nostrils and felt as if God were so near he could talk with him . . . and he did.

God had created life, and it was very good. If you can bask in this scenario for just a few moments, then you will be struck by how great and kind and awesome God is. This is creation as God intended it to be, life to the full. And this is a picture of the eternal life that God has created in our hearts through his Son.

No other being could create like this.

No other god but our God. Elohim.

FIRST-NAME BASIS
For individual or group study

1. In what part of God's creation do you feel his presence most? Why?
2. If you could revisit just one day of the creation as described in Genesis 1, what day would you like to witness and why?
3. What man-made creations most inspire, impress, or amaze you? Why?
4. List the ways in which God has made you a new creation since you became a Christian.
5. If you have not yet professed faith in Christ, what part of your life needs God's creative power in order for you to change? Do you think he can help you change that? Why or why not?
6. In what specific way could you use God's creative power in your life right now?
7. Complete one of these sentences:
   I need to hear what God's Word has to say about . . .
   Right now, I need to feel God's hand in my life in this way. . .
   I wish that God would breathe life into my world by. . .

GETTING ACQUAINTED WITH
ELOHIM

1. Maybe you can take a walk through the woods, sit beside a babbling creek or the banks of a lake, stare out your back window as a storm is rolling in, or contemplate the majesty of a mountain range. Spend an hour simply taking in the evidence of God's creation and pondering how great the God who made all this must truly be.
2. Make a list of the most spectacular natural phenomena you have ever experienced. Thank God for them, meditating on and praising him for his greatness. See Psalm 148.

3. Like the psalmists of long ago, write a song or poem about some details of creation and God's greatness.

4. Little god or big God? This chapter was a reminder that our Creator is a big and powerful God. Write down a big problem you have right now for which there seems to be no solution. Now think big ----- write down three incredible solutions (even if they seem impossible) that God *could* apply to take care of this problem. Spend time in prayer, acknowledging God's greatness and his capabilities. State your desire for his help and state your trust in his ability to act. He's not limited ---- he may create a solution that's even better than the three you thought of!

Jehovah Jireh
Jeh.*ho*.vuh *Jye*.ruh

Jehovah Jireh is not a name God used for himself. Rather, Abraham gave this name to a place because of what God did there. Throughout Scripture we see that God "richly provides" (1 Timothy 6:17).

TWO

PROVIDER
{GENESIS 22:1-19}

CORRIE TEN BOOM

If God sends us on stony paths, he provides strong shoes.

My boys are grown and out of the house now. But when they were in elementary school, we thought it would be fun to become a camping family. It seemed like a good and wholesome way to create family memories at the time; so we bought a tent, some sleeping bags, a camp stove, and other various provisions.

This was only the beginning.

We also decided we would go camping near the Roaring River in Missouri, where we could fish, canoe, hike or just inner-tube downstream. Again, more provisions. Special shoes for wading, shoes for hiking, fishing poles, lures, spinners, and other forms of fish trickery now took up space in my garage. (I bought bait that trusted friends assured me I needed and would work – they were wrong on both counts!) This is not to mention the money spent buying marshmallows, chips, soda, coolers, bug repellent, sunscreen, and all the supplies needed for each excursion.

When all was said and done, it was quite the enterprise to pack up our truck with the necessary provisions each time we headed to the great outdoors for three or four days. Turns out, none of us was very good at catching fish, none of us liked the constant mosquitoes, and we all hated sleeping on the ground in a hot tent. We should have saved the money and gone to a motel with a swimming pool!

What's the point? You just don't head off into the wild without considering all the supplies you will need for the trip. There is nothing worse than getting to your destination only to discover you don't have everything you need for a positive family experience. As it turns out, my family had everything we needed for the trip except the most important thing – a love of camping!

Provisions for a wilderness journey were necessary in the narrative we'll dig into today, found in Genesis 22. And here we discover another descriptive name for God.

A FAITH TEST

An old man (it's not offensive to refer to a man who has lived 115 years as *old*) was taking his teenage son on a camping trip of sorts. I'm conjecturing that the events including Isaac being weaned, Hagar and Ishmael being sent away, and the treaty with Abimelek – all recorded in Genesis 21 – would put Isaac at about fifteen years old at the time.[10]

It would be a three-day journey to their worship destination in the region of Moriah. The man was focused as he loaded his donkey with enough food and, we'll assume, skins of water for the travel party (two servants, his son, and himself; Genesis 22:3). Some sort of tents or at least sleeping mats and blankets were likely added. Some wood, some rope, a fire pot, and a very sharp knife were finally checked off the father's list. Time to go.

Maybe the father's old age had affected his memory, but a major provision was missing for this holy excursion of sacrifice. Or maybe the father knew something that no one else did.

In the first two verses of Genesis 22, God put Abraham's faith to the test. By now the son of promise, Isaac, had grown into young adulthood, and Abraham was contentedly living out his life in a place called Beersheba. He and his wife Sarah, now well along in years, spent every waking minute celebrating the joy of their improbable parenthood. The Lord had blessed them with prosperity and protection from their enemies. Like a retired couple in the twilight of their years, they could simply enjoy the small blessings of daily life while they sat on their porch in the cool of the evening and sipped lemonade (more likely pomegranate juice, but you get the picture).

Abraham and Sarah's faith journey had been long, with many twists and turns. Abraham was seventy-five years old when God told him to leave his home and go to a land that he was going to give him (Genesis 12:1), and Abraham went by faith. God told Abraham that he would be the father of many nations (15:5; 17:5); and though he was old (Hebrews 11:12 says he was "as good as dead") and Sarah was barren, Abraham believed God.

When Abraham was ninety-nine years old, God commanded him to mark their covenant by circumcising all the males in his household (Genesis 17:10; there were 318 trained men at one point – see 14:14), and Abraham obeyed. Not long after this, three visitors came to Abraham's tent for supper, and during this event God promised that Sarah would have a son in the next year. It was hard for Abraham to imagine, but God reasoned, "Is anything too hard for the LORD?" (18:14).

Throughout the years, as far as is recorded, Abraham believed every promise God had made – and they all had come to pass.

This is the point where we can say, "And everyone lived happily ever after," right? Well, not yet. There was still to be another test of faith, another revelation of who God is, and another chance for Abraham to obey. This faith test took place on the mountains of Moriah, where God revealed himself as Jehovah Jireh. Unlike school tests, this test amounted to only one question for Abraham: "How much do you trust me?"

He would either pass or fail.

When I turned forty, a book on manhood and a commercial promoting motorcycling inspired me to buy my first motorcycle (no, it wasn't a midlife crisis… OK, maybe a little). With the help of a friend, I purchased a great bike, but needed the dealership to deliver it to my house due to a couple of minor details: I didn't have a motorcycle license, and I had never ridden a motorcycle in my life!

I enrolled in a motorcycle safety-training course through our local university and spent the next five weeks learning to ride. In no time at all, I was confident in my abilities and was ready for the final class that would determine whether I qualified for a license to operate the machine parked in my garage.

Though I was confident in the skills I had learned, the pressure mounted as the day of the pass/fail test arrived. Soon I would either be labeled "born to ride" or would have to repeat the class. The student before me laid her bike down (that is, she crashed) during one of the easiest skill tests – an automatic fail. What had seemed so easy before now made my palms sweat and my pulse race. The pressure was on.

Fortunately, I passed the test, and I have been riding ever since.

It's fair to say that up to this point Abraham had trusted God. His faith was exemplary. He had trusted God enough to move his family to the unknown land in which he now lived – and God had provided. He had trusted when God showed him the stars and the sand and promised that his descendants would outnumber both.

This man of faith had trusted God enough to circumcise all the males in his household. He had believed that God would give him a son through Sarah – and God had provided the covenant son.

But did he trust the word of the Lord enough to take his son of promise, Isaac, whom he loved, and sacrifice him as a burnt offering? If you can even fathom the possibility, you may be thinking, *Yeah, but Isaac wasn't truly his only son; he still had Ishmael.* While this is true, God had made it clear to Abraham that Isaac was the son through whom he would accomplish his promise and Abraham had already sent Ishmael away (see Genesis 21:8-21). So in Genesis 22:2 this is the test God gave Abraham: How much would he trust God?

> **He had trusted God enough to move his family to the unknown land in which he now lived – and God had provided.**

This faith question is a good one for us to answer as well. How much do *we* trust God?

- Do we trust him with our giving, believing that he will provide for us financially?
- Do we trust him to provide job security when we take a moral stance at our place of employment?
- Do we trust him to provide friendship when we don't give in to the peer pressure around us?
- Do we trust him to provide strength or healing when our health fails?
- Do we trust him to grant us wisdom as we raise our children?
- Do we trust him to provide us with a good Christian spouse when being single is so lonely?
- Do we trust him to provide the answer to our prayers in his timing and way?

- Do we trust him when his expectation seems difficult or even painful?
- Do we trust him when we don't understand what he's up to?

Well, how did you do? Pass or fail? Do your actions align with how you say you trust God? James, the Lord's half-brother tells us, "Faith by itself, if it is not accompanied by action, is dead" (James 2:17). Personally, I find it a lot easier to *say* I trust God to provide than to actually live like it. Maybe that's why God tests us sometimes – to increase our faith in him as Provider!

And Abraham was up to the challenge.

One more thought before we resume our story. What God was asking Abraham to do was beyond any test of faith the one true, living God had ever asked. The pagan gods of Canaan were commonly worshipped through child sacrifice, but not the God of Abraham! *Moloch* was an old Canaanitish idol, called by the Phoenicians and Carthaginians *Melkarth, Baal-melech, Malcom,* and other such names, and related to Baal, a sun-god worshipped, like *Kronos* and *Saturn,* by the sacrifice of children. It was represented by a brazen statute, which was hollow and capable of being heated, and formed with a bull's head, and arms stretched out to receive the children to be sacrificed."[11] God never endorsed or asked for children to be sacrificed to him: in fact, he condemned that practice in the pagan religions: "Do not give any of your children to be sacrificed to Molek" (Leviticus 18:21; see also 20:1-3).

So what gives with this request to sacrifice Isaac? As outside observers after the fact, we readers of Genesis 22 are in on the secret. God was *testing* Abraham. God never intended for Abraham to kill Isaac, but God did intend to see how much Abraham trusted him. If course, Abraham wasn't aware that this was a test. He was simply obeying God's word concerning his son.

GOD HAS PROVIDED

As they set out bright and early, Abraham must have watched as Isaac kissed his mom, assuring her, "Don't worry. We'll be careful. I'll see you in a few days." Maybe Abraham kissed Sarah and added his farewell, and the three-day journey began. We can imagine that as the sun began to set on the first day, Abraham found a suitable place to spend the night, pitched the tents, started a fire, and prepared to rest with a meal. Was the conversation rich, recalling stories and adventures the father and son had experienced together? Or was Abraham quiet? Did he steal away into the night and stare at the stars, asking God, "Are you sure you want me to go through with this plan?" When he lay beside his son and watched him sleep in peace, did a tear slide down his weathered check?

We don't know the details. The Bible tells us only that it took three days to arrive at the designated place of worship. It doesn't take much imagination, however, to deduce that with each day this test must have seemed harder to Abraham and every step brought him agonizingly close to the unthinkable!

Finally, the mountains that God had spoken of came into view. Leaving the servants behind, Abraham led his son to the mountain where they were to worship and Isaac was to be sacrificed. We have only a small part of the conversation between the two of them. It comes in the form of a question. Isaac, being no stranger to worshipping through offering sacrifices to God, asked his father, "Where is the lamb for the burnt offering?" (Genesis 22:7).

Abraham answered honestly, even if he didn't understand fully: "God himself will provide the lamb for the burnt offering, my son" (v. 8). Abraham's answer uses the name we became acquainted with in chapter 1 (Elohim) and pairs it with Jireh – "Elohim Yir'eh, 'God... will provide.'"[12]

What did Abraham mean when he made this confident statement about the impending sacrifice? Again, we can only make some educated guesses. Perhaps Abraham was referring to Isaac as the sacrifice that God had provided. After all, Isaac was a miraculous gift from God. Maybe God had provided this son of promise specifically for this special occasion. We know that God never endorsed child sacrifice, but Abraham was simply obeying him.

Another possible meaning behind Abraham's statement is found in Hebrews 11:19: "Abraham reasoned that God could even raise the dead." The man of faith may have believed that God's provision was Isaac but that God would reward Abraham's obedience by raising his son from the dead. Another possibility is that Abraham had some suspicion that God was testing his trust level and that he would somehow provide a miraculous substitute. That is what God eventually did, but the story doesn't indicate that our main character was aware of the test he was taking.

> **When we are confused about our future, it is helpful to review how God has provided for us in the past.**

The best answer is that Abraham trusted God as Provider because God had always provided before. There had never been a time when God had not provided, and so Abraham's answer was simply that God would provide this time too. He could not have known how or when or in what way this provision would come, but in the midst of the unknowns, he knew firsthand that God had a history of providing. When we are confused about our future, it is helpful to review how God has provided for us in the past.

Our church had just committed to a long-term partnership with a church and pastor in an extremely poor slum in Nairobi, Kenya. Some of our elders and leaders had visited the work, which included a school, an orphanage, a church, and a feeding center in the middle of a shanty village (of thirty thousand people) that had built up over the years on government-owned property. The need was great, and the opportunity for the gospel was greater, so we eagerly followed the Spirit's lead to join the work.

Three months later, some bulldozers showed up unannounced and completely demolished this makeshift village in a matter of hours. The church, school, orphanage, and all living quarters were reduced to a pile of twisted steel, wood, and dirt. Thousands of some of the world's most impoverished people were displaced and had to flee to other places. The pastor was devastated, and so were we when the news arrived. There was literally nothing to show for the many years of hard work, prayer, and faith this pastor and his wife had poured into the work.

They scrambled. They prayed. The teachers found a place under some trees where they could hold classes. The church worshipped in the same location the next day. The pastor and his wife took twenty-two orphans into their own home.

How did they survive in those dark hours? On their knowledge that God had provided so many times in the past, in practical and spiritual ways. The slum had been leveled, but the foundation of their faith in God remained. They prayed for God to provide, even though they had no idea how he might do so. All they knew was that he had provided many times before – surely he would provide again!

A WILLING SACRIFICE

On one of the mountains of Moriah, Abraham and his son built an altar with the wood that Isaac had carried on his back. Somewhere along the way, the father had communicated to his son that *he* was the sacrifice to be offered. We've already established that Isaac was at least fifteen years old at this point. "One thing is very clear: Abraham could not have offered Isaac without Isaac's consent and cooperation. Isaac, as the bearer of the wood, was the stronger of the two. As a young man he was also the quickest and fastest of the two. Apparently Isaac had decided to obey his father whatever the cost, just as his father had decided to obey God whatever the cost."[13] This means that when Abraham bound his son with the rope, Isaac willingly let him do so.

Does that sound like the attitude of the teenage boys you know?

As my boys were growing up, I usually had to bribe them to get them to obey. I remember taking them to an upscale restaurant in Denver when they were ten and seven years old. I had given them at least a hundred speeches about manners, not disrupting other guests, and acting like gentlemen. The promise of a trip to a water park if they behaved was a great incentive, and they were the most obedient young men you could ever care to meet. Several guests and the waiter commented on what "nice young men" they were.

On the way home from the restaurant, they got into a fight in the backseat. Oh well, at least we had a pleasant dinner. I'm sure I could never have given them a large enough incentive to follow me to their own sacrificial deaths.

There is no way to comprehend the emotional strain of this moment for Abraham and Isaac. Tears likely filled the eyes of both father and son as they thought of never seeing each other again. Their hearts pounded faster, the son anticipating death and the father already grieving the loss he would carry to his own grave. I can imagine the scene. Isaac turned his head, exposing his neck where the first cut would be made. Abraham must have had an entire-life-flashing-before-his-eyes moment. Every memory of his son… from his birth to his first steps to teaching him to hunt and tend sheep… all of it flooded the father's memory in an instant.

Knowing the end of the story can cause us to gloss over the intensity of this scene. Have you ever had a well-meaning friend who blurted out the surprise ending to the movie you were going to see? You still might have gone to see the movie, but you missed the thrill of mystery and suspense because you already knew the ending. This is true with the Genesis 22 account of Abraham and Isaac as well. Because the author of Genesis has already told us that this is a test and because we know that Abraham didn't end up actually killing Isaac, we can underplay the emotional duress that Abraham was under. Abraham fully intended to obey God's command. In his heart, he was willing to offer the greatest sacrifice he had ever offered – his only son (see Hebrews 11:17).

MIRACULOUS INTERVENTION

Just as Abraham was about to deliver the deathblow, an angel intervened by calling out his name twice. Abraham responded to the voice, and God spoke through the angel, "Do not lay a hand on the boy,' he said. 'Do not do anything to him. Now I know that you fear God, because you have not withheld from me your son, your only son'" (Genesis 22:12).

And just like that, the drama was over. Abraham took the knife meant for sacrifice and used it to cut the ropes that bound Isaac. Surely they embraced wept, laughed, shouted for joy, and danced in worship.

With all the excitement, perhaps they hadn't noticed a ram caught in a nearby bush. Then Abraham spotted the sacrifice that would take his son's place. God's direct provision. Abraham said that God would provide, and he had.

Abraham then proceeded to sacrifice this ram on the altar that he had prepared for his son, designating the place with the name that reveals an important aspect of God's nature: Jehovah Jireh. "The LORD Will Provide" (v. 14). This name identifies the God that Isaac and Abraham experienced on the mountains of Moriah that day.

By faith, the pastor and his wife from Kenya proceeded to meet with government officials, reorganized their school, cared for the orphans, and traveled to the United States with tickets we had already purchased before that catastrophic Saturday. As a church, our intent was to encourage them, nurture their souls, give them some physical rest, and bless them with a gift for their work. We had been told that $40,000 would help them rebuild a more permanent structure for a church, school, and orphanage. Once the government had given them permission and assurances, they could rebuild. The leaders of our church prayed that God might use our congregation to bless this newly formed ministry partnership.

On the Sunday the pastor and his wife visited with us, we situated our announcements at the end of the services so that we could introduce our new fellow laborers from Kenya. After a moving video that showed footage of the destroyed slum and the resiliency of the church there, we brought the pastor and his wife onstage to a standing ovation. Then I challenged our people to give – in one offering – the $40,000 to meet the needs of these brothers and sisters an ocean away. We had already taken up our regular offering on that Sunday; this was a gift above and beyond that, to be collected by the ushers as the people went out. Our prayer was that God would provide generously through his people.

And he did.

Later that evening at an event designed for our congregation to get to know the Kenyan couple and their work, the offering total was revealed. Our mission pastor held us in suspense for a moment, then announced the total for the rebuilding work in Kenya: $196,000! Spontaneous worship happened. We clapped, then we cried, then we high-fived, then we hugged… and offered a thousand "Praise Gods!" It was truly one of the most spirit-filled moments in my life.

Needless to say, our new pastor friend was overwhelmed. He literally fell to the ground in praise. Two months earlier, he could not possibly have seen beyond the destruction of many years of ministry and work. But the God he served is Jehovah Jireh. This God was working ahead, and he provided in a miraculous way once again! (Over the next week, the offering total would rise to $225,000 as further donations came in.)

GOD STILL PROVIDES

Sometimes we look at Abraham's story and hear stories like the one from Kenya and wonder why *we* don't receive from the Provider like that. At the same time, we acknowledge that we don't really desire faith tests like Abraham and this Kenyan church faced! The reality, though, is that God decides the tests and how he will provide for each person. Sometimes while God is giving his provisions to us and is testing us, we fail to recognize his hand. We don't always grasp how he is growing our faith through specific tests in our lives.

God still provides for us in practical ways. Jesus tells us in the sermon recorded in Matthew's Gospel that God supplied the essentials of life: "He causes his sun to rise on the evil and the good, and sends rain on the righteous and the unrighteous" (Matthew 5:45). Later, James wrote, "Every good and perfect gift is from above, coming down from the Father of the heavenly lights" (James 1:17). God's provision reaches to feeding all the birds and dressing all the flowers (Matthew 6:25-30). When Abraham thought of God in terms of "the Lord will provide," he was talking about the ram in the thicket. But he was also pointing to every good thing you and I enjoy on this earth. Every sunrise, every smile, every morsel of food, and every breath we take is a provision from the Father.

In the Scriptures we find other examples of Jehovah Jireh in action, like these:

- He provided food for Elijah near the brook of the Kerith Ravine by directing ravens to bring bread and meat to the prophet every morning and every evening (1 Kings 17:1-6).
- He provided some extra daylight so that Joshua and the armies of Israel could triumph over the five kings of the Amorites (Joshua 10:5, 12-14).
- He provided a way through the Red Sea when the Israelites had no way out as the Egyptians pursued them (Exodus 14:21, 22).

God sometimes provides today by means of his miraculous power as well.

From time to time at our church we offer a healing invitation during our Sunday worship services. We obey the simple instructions taught in the book of James and invite people to come and be anointed with oil (we use olive oil) and prayed over by the elders of our church for healing (James 5:14, 15). There is always a large response.

In the last couple of years, we have seen people healed of cancer, depression, chronic headaches, high blood pressure, epileptic seizures, and numerous other physical illnesses and limitations. So we believe that God still provides physical healing, though he doesn't choose to heal in every situation. For reasons we don't fully understand, God doesn't answer every prayer the way we would like. (We'll talk more about this in the next chapter.) Regardless, we always trust him as Provider.

God also continues to provide through his people, the church, in a variety of ways. Even though much of our culture clings to an unfair perception of the worldwide church as corrupt and hypocritical, the church continues to bless millions of lives worldwide by providing for practical needs through missions, Christian relief organizations, and the philanthropy of individual believers. For example:

- Many may wonder why God doesn't provide for the poor Christians in Haiti, but I saw firsthand as God provided richly through his church during the earthquake of 2010.
- Some may question why God allows a "good" person to lose his job, but I've seen Jehovah Jireh provide clothes, cars, houses, food, and money through a person's loving congregation.
- Some may ask how God could allow the sudden death of a young person, but I have witnessed how the intense sympathy of Christian people has served to spiritually relieve the pain of those who have endured this tragedy.

In these ways and many more, Jehovah Jireh continues to live up to his description.

PHYSICAL AND SPIRITUAL PROVISION

Abraham and Isaac felt especially blessed to sacrifice in worship the ram God provided for the burnt offering. After their mountaintop experience, they did not leave the mountain wondering about the future. God spoke again through the angel, reiterating the covenant he had made with Abraham in Genesis 12, 15 and 17: "I swear by myself, declared the LORD, that because you have done this and have not withheld your son, your only son, I will surely bless you… and through your offspring all nations on earth will be blessed" (22:16-18).

Abraham could begin his return home to Beersheba, trusting that God would continue to live up to his reputation as Jehovah Jireh and would provide for his future needs, as well as those of his descendants.

Abraham and Isaac made their way back to the camp where they had left the servants. I imagine this exchange:

"Did you meet with God on the mountain as you wished, my master?" one of the men asked Abraham.

"You have no idea," Abraham answered, as he winked at Isaac with a smile.

We can assume that the mood was light on the return journey, and in a short three days, they were reunited with Sarah. I've always wondered how they broke the news to her about the Moriah experience. Maybe Isaac joked, "Dad almost killed me, Mom… seriously!" Or maybe Abraham began his account with: "Sarah, you know how I've said we must always obey God? Well, you may not believe this, but…" However these two related the story, it became part of the historic fiber of the Old Testament people of God and a reminder of the God who provides.

God did continue to provide in Abraham's life.

- When he faced the test of his wife's death in Genesis 23, God provided a place of burial through the generosity of the Hittite neighbors.
- When Abraham wanted to find a suitable wife for his son in Genesis 24, God provided the beautiful Rebekah.

- When Abraham remarried at an old age in Genesis 25, God provided him with more children.
- God granted Abraham sixty years of life after this Moriah faith test, each day filled with countless provisions for Abraham's welfare.
- Even after the patriarch's death, we find God blessing Abraham's son Isaac in Genesis 25:11. (God blessed Abraham's son Ishmael too.)

God said that through Abraham's descendants all nations on earth would be blessed, and that includes us! The apostle Paul spent a good amount of time tying the New Testament people of faith, the church, to the promise that God made to Abraham. Paul assured all Christ followers: "If you belong to Christ, then you are Abraham's seed, and heirs according to the promise" (Galatians 3:29). The spiritual provision that God made for all mankind is salvation through Jesus Christ. Paul said, "The promises were spoken to Abraham and to his seed. Scripture does not say 'and to seeds' meaning many people, but 'and to your seed,' meaning one person, who is Christ" (v. 16). In Jesus Christ, Jehovah Jireh provides his people not with the material blessings of land, prosperity, children and protection he did Abraham. Instead he provides something much greater! "Praise be to the God and Father of our Lord Jesus Christ, who has blessed us in the heavenly realms with every spiritual blessing in Christ" (Ephesians 1:3).

God did this by providing a spotless Lamb, a substitutionary sacrifice, for our sins. Can you fathom that as God was testing Abraham to offer his only son as a sacrifice, he knew that there would come another day centuries later when God would offer his one and only perfect Son on the hill of Golgotha and take away the sins of the world? The comparisons between the two dramatic events are remarkable:

- Isaac was Abraham's only son, and Jesus was God's only Son.
- Isaac carried the wood up the mountain, and Jesus carried his cross up the hill.

- Isaac was a son of promise, and Jesus was the promised one to come.
- Isaac submitted to his father's will in sacrifice, and Jesus prayed to the Father, "Not my will, but yours be done" (Luke 22:42).
- A ram became the substitute for Isaac, and Jesus the Lamb became a substitute for us.
- Abraham did not withhold his son, and God did not withhold his Son.

Many Bible scholars have worked hard to identify the place of Jesus' crucifixion as being close to the location of Abraham's place of sacrifice. Scripture does indicate that Mt. Moriah was the place where the temple was built (2 Chronicles 3:1), and we know Jesus was crucified close by.

I'm not sure that it matters. What matters is that, like Isaac, we were destined to die (because of our sin), but God provided a substitute. Though Jesus could have called on thousands of angels to take him off the cross, an angel did not stop the sacrifice of God's Son. God provided a way for us to be saved, and this is the greatest provision of all. God is Jehovah Jireh, and the sacrifice of his Son, Jesus, confirms it!

FIRST-NAME BASIS
For individual or group study

1. As a student did you prefer true-false, multiple choice, or essay tests? Why?
2. What event or period of your life has seemed as if God were testing you? Explain.
3. Think of a time when God provided for you in an unexpected way. On a scale of 1 to 10, chart your faith before and after this provision.
4. What, if anything, is God doing in your life these days that doesn't seem to make sense? How can you pray effectively about it?
5. If God were to ask you to take your most valuable possession (or relationship) up a mountain and sacrifice it to him, what would that be? What would be your response?

GETTING ACQUAINTED WITH
JEHOVAH JIREH

1. Abraham named the place of sacrifice on Mt. Moriah "The LORD Will Provide." If you could assign the name Jehovah Jireh to some actual locations from your life history, what places come to mind? What significant events happened there? How did God provide in each of those situations? If geographically possible, revisit one of those places for a time of reflection, prayer, and thanksgiving.
2. Spend a week charting God's provision in your life. Begin by listing some areas in which you feel like you don't fully trust God. (You may draw from the list at the beginning of this chapter, page 33.) After you have identified two or three areas for growth, use a Bible concordance to identify Scriptures that speak to these. Note what the Bible says about each, and then commit to a half hour of prayer for

each specific area over the next several days. Declare to God your desire to trust his provision in these areas. Finally, record any provision you observe and thank Jehovah Jireh for his work in your life.

3. Write a letter to yourself in which you note specific areas in which you need God's provision. Do not limit your list to physical things, but think about spiritual provision as well. Seal the letter in an envelope, then give it to someone you trust, instructing that person to return it to you in six months. At that time you will be able to review the letter and celebrate by thanking God for specific ways in which he has provided for you.

Jehovah Rophe
Jeh.*hovuh Rah*.fah

More literally, this name is "Jehovah, the one healing." The
prophet Jeremiah understood that God was the true Healer.
He said, "Heal me, LORD, and I will be healed" (17:14).

THREE

HEALER
{EXODUS 15:26; NUMBERS 21:1-9}

PHILIP YANCEY

---

*I find cries of lament penciled long ago in the margins of my Bible and give
thanks that I made it through that particular valley... Remembering my
relationship with God takes effort and intentionality. I cannot pull out a home
video and watch our history and growth together; there are no photo albums
of living in faith. I must consciously work at reviewing both the progress of the
ache and the progress of the healing.*

I had not been out of Bible college for more than a month when
a woman in my first full-time ministry (a lady we'll call Cindy)
was diagnosed with stage 4 breast cancer. This was particularly
devastating because Cindy and her family were deeply loved by

everyone in this Midwest church. Her husband served as a Sunday school teacher and deacon. They had two small children, and Cindy was very involved in the children's ministry.

But the cancer was advanced, and the prognosis was not good. Doctors were recommending a double mastectomy followed by intense chemotherapy and radiation treatments (cancer treatments were much less advanced twenty-five years ago). Even with this aggressive treatment, Cindy was given two to three months to live. But before she began the treatment, she asked the elders and some of the church staff to pray for her healing.

Honestly, I had never been a part of this kind of prayer before. While the churches I grew up in believed that God could heal, they just didn't lean toward the miraculous. While there was often prayer for a sick person to get well, many simply didn't expect God's visible, divine intervention. In my opinion, these good Christian people simply were not inclined to believe that God healed in the same way he did in the Bible. Maybe they were afraid of that kind of Holy Spirit evidence in their midst, or they were cautious toward the abuses of spiritual manifestations that some denominations had fallen into. Regardless, I had never before witnessed anyone being anointed with oil while being prayed over.

But Cindy asked for the elders to function in a biblical way, and they did. The Bible provides this directive: "Is anyone among you sick? Let them call the elders of the church to pray over them and anoint them with oil in the name of the Lord. And the prayer offered in faith will make the sick person well" (James 5:14, 15).

We gathered in the senior pastor's office for this intense time of prayer, and honestly, my faith wasn't that strong. I didn't expect Cindy to be physically healed. I believed she *could*; it's just that my unbelief outweighed the belief, I guess.

While the passage in the book of James tells us what to do, it doesn't give much detail concerning the *how*. So the senior pastor directed as he was led by the Spirit.

When the participants all arrived, a large square of plastic had been placed on the floor and a bottle of olive oil on the desk. When Cindy arrived, a short update on her condition was given, and then she confessed that she believed that God could heal her. Within minutes, she was kneeling as we gathered around and laid hands on her to pray for healing. Our pastor was pouring the bottle of oil on her head (yeah, the whole bottle... very untidy).

"In Jesus' name, we ask for you to heal Cindy, Lord," the prayers began. The oil covered her hair and dripped down onto her clothes. At first I was thinking, *Man, her clothes are ruined.* Then it became a spiritually moving experience. Men prayed through tears and broken voices. All our hands were now slippery and trembling while we prayed as sincerely as we could for the cancer to be taken away.

If no healing had taken place, I would still count this as one of the most Holy Spirit-filled moments in my ministry. But something wonderful happened beyond the great prayers offered and the faith that was exhibited. Cindy said that as we prayed she felt a strange heat starting from her head and flowing down her entire body. She was deeply moved, and her faith moved me.

Three days later she went to the doctor for some more tests and preparation for surgery. The tests showed no signs of cancer! They ran more tests and called in more experts. A week earlier Cindy had cancer, but every test now indicated that she was cancer free. Many speculated that the original tests had given false results or that some doctor had misread them, but everyone who had prayed for her knew exactly what had happened. God miraculously healed Cindy from cancer!

HEALING THE WATER

The children of Israel had just been delivered from Egypt in spectacular fashion. God had led the estimated two to three million people through the Red Sea on dry ground and had drowned the Egyptian army in that same sea as they pursued. Moses and his sister

Miriam led a worship service that included songs, tambourines, and dancing – praising God for his miraculous work (Exodus 15). The celebration surely continued for some time as they traveled away from Egypt.

Then they wandered into the Desert of Shur looking for water, but didn't find any. "When they came to Marah, they could not drink its water because it was bitter. (That is why the place is called Marah)" (v. 23). Now the praise songs of deliverance had completely faded. Their physical thirst overwhelmed the spiritual refreshment they had recently experienced. The people of God did what any self-respecting group of God's people do when things become unclear – they complained ("grumbled," according to v. 24). Isn't it amazing how fast we sometimes go from praising to complaining?

The people grumbled to Moses, and Moses cried out to God. We aren't told how the communication between God and his leader took place. Maybe Moses moved away from the sound of the griping voices to pray, or maybe he simply lifted his head to the skies and passed the complaint heavenward. Whatever the mode, Moses talked to God, and God gave him direction. Maybe something like this:

"Moses."

"Yes, Lord."

"Do you see that piece of wood Aaron is sitting on?"

"Yes."

"Pick it up and throw it into the water."

"But Lord, what good will that… OK, I'll do it."

Their physical thirst overwhelmed the spiritual refreshment they had recently experienced.

The Bible tells us that Moses threw the wood into the water, and "the waters were made sweet" (v. 25, *KJV*). God had "healed" the bitter water and made it drinkable for the thirsty millions in the desert.

Then, using this miracle as an object lesson, God introduced himself by another name. He said, "If you listen carefully to the LORD your God and do what is right in his eyes, if you pay attention to his commands and keep all his decrees, I will not bring on you any of the diseases I brought on the Egyptians, for I am the LORD, who heals you" (v. 26). God was essentially asking them, "Are you impressed with how I healed the bitter waters and made them drinkable?" He continued, "Healing is what I do. In fact, healing is one of my names. You can call me Jehovah Rophe."

THE NEED FOR HEALING

Do you need healing? I think I know the answer. Of course you do! You may be in need of physical healing. Like the lady from my first church, you may be in the midst of chemotherapy or radiation treatment for cancer right now. Have you endured surgeries for broken bones, corrective vision, heart bypass, ligament repairs, or dental work? Maybe you were born with serious physical limitations and have lived a life of pain. Do you experience daily headaches, stomach pains, or dizziness? I'm guessing, of course, but a general understanding of the human condition makes it an educated one.

Our physical bodies will suffer a variety of painful conditions. Like the Israelites coming to the waters of Marah, all of us eventually experience the bitter drink of physical pain.

Some people may not be suffering physically right now; their ailments are mental or emotional in nature. There has been a rise in the frequency of autism among children. Many people deal with paralyzing depression, unable to function relationally with family or friends. Others live with serious phobias that involve being around crowds, worrying about the future, or fear of failure. Many have faced such abusive and traumatic experiences that they ae unable to allow themselves to invest in relationships.

Finally, all of us need healing of the most significant kind. We suffer from the most destructive malady of all: sin. There is no way to truly quantify the effects of sin on our world and our lives, but the apostle Paul described it pretty well in his letter to the Roman Christians, when he spoke of creation's "bondage to decay" (Romans 8:21). He went on to say, "We know that the whole creation has been groaning as in the pains of childbirth right up to the present time" (v. 22). Two millennia later we are still groaning from our sin.

- Our selfishness leads to anger toward those who have what we want.
- Our lust leads to a variety of sexual expressions but causes us to miss true intimacy.
- Our lying leads us to distrust others.
- Our greed leads to our discontent.
- Our disrespect for the well-being of others causes us to devalue life.
- Our shallow focus on physical attributes leaves us insecure about who we are.
- Our worship of ourselves leaves us feeling helpless when spiritual power is what is requires.

When God told Adam and Eve that to eat from the tree of knowledge of good and evil meant death (Genesis 2:17), he wasn't speaking only of physically dying. This world is suffering from the spiritual disease of sin, and it is terminal.

Well, that was pretty depressing, huh? No matter how you slice it, we live in a sick world. If you couldn't relate to any of the physical, mental, emotional, or spiritual diseases mentioned above, you probably aren't being completely honest with yourself. You need healing and don't even know it! On the other hand, if you could relate to one or several of the conditions listed, then there is good news for you. There is a God who heals. His name as revealed to the Israelites in the desert is Jehovah Rophe – and his healing is more than physical.

"The verb from which *rophe* is derived occurs sixty-seven times in the Old Testament. Though it often refers to physical healing, it usually has a larger meaning as well, involving the entire person... God also heals sin... The Hebrew Scriptures, in fact, link sickness and sin by presenting sin as the cause of illness just as it is the cause of death."[14] You can see this attitude expressed by Jesus' disciples in their question concerning a man who was blind. "Rabbi," they asked, "who sinned, this man or his parents, that he was born blind?" (John 9:2). We'll talk more of Jesus' healing in a moment, but first let's look at another story of complaining and healing from the history of God's people. It's found in the book of Numbers.

A SIGN OF HEALING

Fast-forward nearly forty years from the healing of the bitter waters at Marah. The sojourn of punishment in the desert was mercifully coming to an end. Moses was nearing the end of his journey, having already forfeited his opportunity to lead the people into the promised land because of his disobedience to God (see Numbers 20:12). Moses' brother and high priest, Aaron, had recently died (v. 28).

"When the Canaanite king of Arad, who lived in the Negev, heard that Israel was coming along the road to Atharim, he attacked the Israelites and captured some of them" (21:1). God faithfully came to their rescue and delivered them from this pagan king. However, it wasn't much farther into the journey before the children of Israel were complaining – again. "They spoke against God and against Moses, and said, 'Why have you brought us up out of Egypt to die in the wilderness? There is no bread! There is no water! And we detest this miserable food!'" (v. 5).

Like high school students in the cafeteria, they complained mostly about the food.

I suppose they were tired of manna. I get it. Seriously, how many ways can you prepare even "heavenly" bread? Every tabernacle pitch-in dinner, it was the same old manna casserole. On summer outings, it was always manna patties on the grill. For breakfast, manna flakes cereal. The menu was predictable: ba-manna pudding, manna-roni and cheese, mannana bread and MLT's (manna, lettuce and tomato sandwiches)! This travel-weary group was simply tired of manna.

But once again, isn't it ironic how humans often end up complaining about the blessings of God? Complaining about God's provision is equal to complaining about God. Remember in the last chapter how God provided a ram for the sacrifice? What if Abraham or Isaac had complained that it was a ram instead of a bull? I'm sure Isaac was just glad to have a substitute!

God doesn't take too kindly to the ungratefulness of those he blesses, and often this leads to his discipline. In this case, he sent venomous snakes among the complainers. The snakes "bit the people and many Israelites died" (v. 6).

Sometimes our pain comes from our own foolish and sinful choices, from following our own selfish appetites instead of trusting in God to take care of our needs. For example:

- Many have selfishly rebelled against their families and live with the pain of separation and family turmoil.
- Some suffer from the emotional regret of having had an abortion at an earlier age.
- Others suffer from the scars of their sexual promiscuity during young adult years and the feelings of guilt that continue long into adulthood.
- Some have lost family, job, friends, and health due to drug or alcohol addictions.
- Others have forfeited friendships by repeated lying and deception to those closest to them.
- Some have literally bankrupted themselves financially because of their own greed and coveting.

- Still others carry the punishment and stigma that followed their decision to break the law.
- Many face the painful reality of being estranged from their grown children because they ignored the children when they were young, in exchange for pursuing a career.
- Others have mentally, physically, or emotionally abused those closest to them and, though they want forgiveness, feel as though there is no hope of reconciliation.

For every sin we commit, there is a consequence. When we go against God, we bring pain into our lives. Some people feel the sting of their sin just as the Israelites felt the painful bites of the serpents in the desert. Others are just sure that it is only a matter of time before their sins find them out, so they exist in a state of spiritual paranoia.

Is there a cure for this plague of sin that separates us from God? There is, and it begins with repentance.

As the snakes slithered from tent to tent inflicting painful bites, the Israelites realized God was punishing them for speaking against him and his provision. They repented. "The people came to Moses and said, 'We sinned when we spoke against the LORD and against you. Pray that the LORD will take the snakes away from us'" (Numbers 21:7).

I've always wondered if Moses was ever tempted to refuse one of their requests. It appears that he was often frustrated with these "stiff-necked" and "rebellious" people (see Deuteronomy 31:27), but he also seems to have loved them enough to speak to God on their behalf. In this case, Moses prayed for God to deliver the Israelites from the plague of snakes.

God answered this prayer by directing Moses to make a symbol of healing. "The LORD said to Moses, 'Make a snake and put it up on a pole; anyone who is bitten can look at it and live.' So Moses made a bronze snake and put it up on a pole" (Numbers 21:8, 9). This symbol became the Lord's tool for healing the snake-bitten people of God, and so represented his name Jehovah Rophe.

THE SIGN STILL STANDS FOR HEALING

The ancient world gives us at least two symbols with some variation of a snake and a pole related to medicine and healing. These symbols can be readily seen on doors, buildings, signs, doctors' coats, and websites of many medical institutions. The next time you go to your doctor's office, hospital, or clinic, look for either the caduceus or Asclepius symbol. Dr. Keith Blayney explains the historical difference:

Many "medical" organisations use a symbol of a short rod entwined by two snakes and topped by a pair of wings, which is actually the caduceus or magic wand of the Greek god Hermes (Roman Mercury), messenger of the gods…

Professional and patient centred organisations (such as the NZMA, in fact most medical Associations around the world including the World Health Organization) use the "correct" and traditional symbol of medicine, the staff of Asclepius with a single serpent encircling a staff, classically a rough-hewn knotty tree limb. Asclepius (an ancient Greek physician deified as the god of medicine) is traditionally depicted as a bearded man wearing a robe that leaves his chest uncovered and holding a staff with his sacred single serpent coiled around it.[15]

There is no evidence that the snake Moses constructed of bronze in the desert became the universal symbol of medicine that we recognize today. We do know, however, that this event in Hebrew history predates the rise of the Greek civilization and, therefore, the "god physician" Asclepius by at least nine hundred years.

We also know that the Israelite people turned this healing pole into a god that they worshipped. When Hezekiah became king of Judah, eliminating this god was part of his attempt to turn the people back to God. "He broke into pieces the bronze snake Moses had made, for up to that time the Israelites had been burning incense to it. (It was called Nehushtan)" (2 Kings 18:4).

This means that eight hundred years after the healing from

snakebites in the desert, this symbol of healing still remained as a god (albeit a false god) of healing to many of the Hebrew people. Though I cannot prove this historically, I suggest it is at least a possibility that some of the Greek mythology associated with the healing snake and pole was copied from this biblical incident.

LIFTED UP FOR ALL TO SEE

Of course, the symbol itself wasn't what healed the people. The obedient act of looking up to the raised image as God had commanded initiated Jehovah Rophe's healing power. Imagine the desert scene as it may have happened in real life. Somewhere near Moses' tent he (or perhaps one of his aides) held high a standard with the image of the snake. Not far away, in the camp of the tribe of Issachar, a young boy surrounded by some of his playmates was drawing in the sand with a stick. Silently, a serpent came up from behind and, with venomous fangs, struck him on the leg. The children scattered with screams as the boy shrieked in pain. His mother, seeing the fresh wound, scooped him into her arms and quickly made her way to the place of healing. Already the wound was red, and the boy's foot had begun to swell. The cries of the boy got louder as the pain increased.

"Look at the snake," The mother instructed, turning his head firmly with her free hand. The little boy gazed upward through tear-filled eyes and looked at an image of the very thing that had caused him pain. The pain subsided. The child lived. He had been healed by the Lord as he looked to the symbol the Lord had prescribed.

Moses continued to hold the symbol high for all to see. As the people looked up in hope and obedience, the God of Israel brought healing to them.

God is a healing God. He may have used this episode of raising up a snake to illustrate how he would someday raise up his Son to bring healing. Jesus himself made this connection. In a conversation with the Jewish teacher Nicodemus, Jesus alluded to himself as the "lifted up" Healer. "Just as Moses lifted up the snake in the wilderness, so the Son of Man must be lifted up, that everyone who believes may have eternal life in him" (John 3:14, 15).

JESUS AS HEALER

As Jehovah Rophe in the flesh, it is not surprising that Jesus, the Son of Man, came as Healer. Toward the beginning of his ministry, we catch a glimpse of the extent and magnitude of the kind of healing that would accompany Jesus' ministry. After he had been rejected in his hometown of Nazareth, as recorded in Luke 4:28-30, he made his way to Capernaum on the shores of Galilee. His ministry began with a sermon in the synagogue that was interrupted by a demon-possessed man. With authority, Jesus commanded the evil spirit to come out of him; and it did, leaving the man spiritually and emotionally healed (vv. 31-37).

Leaving the synagogue, Jesus came to the home of Simon Peter's mother-in-law, who was sick with some kind of fever. Jesus went to her and spoke sternly to the fever ("rebuked" is the word Luke uses), and she was healed. In fact, she felt so much better, she got up and started making dinner (vv. 38, 39).

Meanwhile, the buzz about Jesus healing in the synagogue had spread throughout the entire village and surrounding areas. "At sunset, the people brought to Jesus all who had various kinds of sickness" (v. 40). Those who were ill, those with family members or friends who were sick, and those who just wanted to catch a glimpse of this miracle man flooded into Capernaum in search of Jesus.

Can you imagine this crazy scene? I picture paralyzed people on mats carried by friends, as beggars afflicted with blindness groped around and cried out for healing. Little children at death's door lay limp in their fathers' arms. Those possessed by demons were being restrained by family members, as they lashed out with both physical and verbal aggression. Those afflicted with leprosy stood at a distance, inching dangerously close to the crowd while trying to maintain their lawful distance. Perhaps every sick person within a day's walking distance stood outside the house, in hopes of being healed. Like an overcrowded emergency room during a natural disaster, those who were sick, in pain, and filled with desperation packed into the town of Capernaum.

What would Jesus do?

"Laying his hands on each one, he healed them. Moreover, demons came out of many people shouting, 'You are the Son of God!' But he rebuked them and would not allow them to speak, because they knew he was the Messiah" (vv. 40, 41). Jesus blessed every sick person there with his healing touch. "Each one." The Son of God, as the embodiment of Jehovah Rophe, lived up to his name by curing every disease, casting out every demon, drying every tear, and restoring everyone who was ill to complete health. Can you imagine the celebration in the town of Capernaum as literally every illness was eradicated for at least one day? These details aren't mentioned in the book of Luke, just the healing event itself.

Jesus himself had said that the coming of the Messiah could be identified by his ministry of healing. When some disciples of John the Baptist approached Jesus to confirm that he was the one who was to come, he was in the middle of another heal fest. "At that very time Jesus cured many who had diseases, sickness and evil spirits, and gave sight to many who were blind" (Luke 7:21).

In light of all this healing, the disciples' question probably didn't need a verbal response, but Jesus referred to Isaiah's prophecy about the one who would come. "See he replied to the messengers, 'Go back and report to John what you have seen and heard: The blind receive sight, the lame walk, those who have leprosy are cleansed, the deaf hear, the dead are raised, and the good news is proclaimed to the poor'" (v. 22). In other words, "I'm the one!"

What conclusions can we make about the healing found in the ministry of Jesus?

- God the Healer, introduced by name to the Israelites in Exodus 15:26, came to earth to bring physical healing via the life of Jesus.
- There is no disease, illness, or sickness we currently experience that God through Jesus cannot heal.
- Even the suffering caused by Satan and his demonic attacks on the minds and souls of people is under the authority of God's command and within his ability to heal.
- Looking to God in faith, obedience, and repentance is the only hope we have for physical and spiritual healing.

JESUS AS RESCUER

Ultimately Jesus didn't come only to bring physical healing. Just as the brazen serpent was given as a sign of the healing God was willing to give, so Jesus' physical healing was a sign of spiritual healing only he could give.

The Gospel writers used an interesting word for *save* in their telling of the life of Jesus. It is the Greek word *sozo*, and it literally means "to save" or "to rescue"; but depending on the context, it can also be translated as *heal or make whole*.[16]

Not surprisingly, the physician Luke used this word in both ways. He used it (or different forms of it) to signify salvation in the eternal, spiritual sense: "Today *salvation* has come to this house, because this man, too, is the son of Abraham. For the Son of Man came to seek and to *save* the lost" (Luke 19:9, 10). Luke also used this word to speak of healing in the physical sense: "Then he said to her, 'Daughter, your faith has *healed* you. Go in peace'" (8:48). Two verses later Luke recorded Jesus' words to Jairus about his sick daughter: "Don't be afraid; just believe, and she will be *healed*" (8:50, emphasis added in all).

This has led some theologians to conclude that the physical healings performed by Jesus were tied to the spiritual salvation found only in him. "This shows that there is some link between the healings brought by Jesus and the spiritual salvation which He brought to men, a link which is not merely linguistically easy but has its deeper roots in the fact that common to both sets of activity is the power of God revealed in Jesus in response to faith. The power to heal and the authority to save both reside in God."[17] Yes, the healing promised by God when he revealed himself as Jehovah Rophe was displayed in his ability to physically heal from the venom of a snakebite, but ultimately it was fulfilled in the power to spiritually heal a sin-sick world.

THE ULTIMATE SYMBOL OF HEALING

In the end, the Jewish leaders were jealous of all the attention and authority the crowds bestowed on the healer, Jesus from Nazareth. Just as God's people in the time of Moses failed to acknowledge God's provision of food, the Jews in Jesus' time failed to recognize God's provision of "the living bread that came down from heaven" (John 6:51). Eventually, most of those who had been healed by him rejected him, denied him, betrayed him, and shouted for him to be crucified. The Roman governor gave the orders, and the soldiers nailed him to a cross. In a place called Skull Hill, they raised him up for all to see. And they looked on.

- "The people stood watching" (Luke 23:35).
- "The rulers even sneered at him" (v. 35) as they looked on.
- The soldiers joined in the mockery as they watched: "If you are the king of the Jews, save yourself" (v. 37).
- The criminal on one side questioned him, "Aren't you the Messiah? Save yourself and us!" (v. 39).

- The criminal on the other side looked at Jesus and asked to be remembered (v. 42).
- The centurion saw and then said, "Surely this was a righteous man" (v. 47).
- Those who witnessed it all "beat their breasts and went away" (v. 48).
- "All those who knew him... stood at a distance, watching these things" (v. 49).

What no one fully grasped was that the cross of Jesus was the sign of the healing they all desperately needed. Only by looking to the cross and the work accomplished through Jesus there could mankind ultimately be healed of all the pain and suffering this world offers. This is why the prophet had declared seven hundred years before, "By his wounds we are healed" (Isaiah 53:5). On the cross Jesus took the pain of sin on himself so that those who suffer from sin's effects could be healed eternally. It is here that Jehovah Rophe performed his greatest healing of all.

Through the cross of Jesus, Jehovah Rophe still heals physically, but I believe he does his greatest healing in the spiritual realm. At our church, we regularly offer an invitation for healing at the end of our services. Our elders stand ready with vials of oil, and we pray over dozens of people who come forward to be healed of all sorts of things.

> **What no one fully grasped was that the cross of Jesus was the sign of the healing they all desperately needed.**

On one of these occasions, a couple came forward to ask for healing in their marriage after a long and secret struggle concerning the wife's infidelity and the husband's anger. With tear-filled eyes they made their way down the center aisle, and we embraced. The request was simple. "We need God to miraculously heal our marriage," the husband whispered. I dabbed oil on both hands and smeared it on each of their foreheads as I begged God to bring unity and love into their relationship.

Months later, in separate conversations, both marriage partners testified how they left church that morning with a new peace and extreme confidence that God would bless their desire to keep their marriage vows. Each confessed that bitterness had been replaced by hope, and hurt feelings had instantly been washed away with a renewed love for one another. In one prayer their entire outlook and attachment to one another had changed. They still had some communication issues to resolve through counseling, but God had healed them. Eventually, they shared their testimony with their grown kids and their close Christian friends. Still today, only a few people know that behind this great Christian marriage is the miraculous answer to that morning's prayer. Jehovah Rophe had healed their marriage.

He healed them, he has healed many others, and he can heal you too!

FIRST-NAME BASIS
For individual or group study

1. Do you know someone who has gone through or is currently experiencing considerable pain? (Remember this can be physical, mental, emotional, or spiritual suffering.) In what ways would that person say God has sustained him or her during this difficult time?

2. What is the most serious medical situation you have ever faced personally? How did you deal with it?

3. Describe a recent visit to a medical professional and the remedy prescribed for your healing. Did it work? Or describe an illness, disease, or injury from which you no longer suffer. How did you get well? What lingering effects remain today from this experience?

4. If you were to assign a number to your sins (as we do to measure cancer in stages) before you came to faith in Jesus, would you have been a stage 1, 2, 3, or 4? Explain your answer.

5. Using words associated with healing (like *scars, symptoms, pain, remission,* and *full recovery*), describe how you have personally benefited from what Jesus accomplished on the cross.

GETTING ACQUAINTED WITH
JEHOVAH ROPHE

1. Call the elders of your church and ask them to anoint you with oil and pray over you for a specific rescue. This might be for a physical, spiritual, or emotional healing. Some specific examples might include healing for a marriage, healing from cancer, healing from pain of sins committed against you, or healing from a recurring sin you struggle with.

2. Contact your pastor or someone at your church who can supply you with a list of those from your church who are shut-in or in the hospital. Volunteer to visit several of those on the list. As you visit each one, spend some time talking with them, reading Scriptures of healing to them, and praying for them (it's nice to hold the person's hand as you pray). Imagine yourself as the instrument of healing in the hand of Jehovah Rophe as you visit each person.

3. Ask a local soup kitchen in your community if you or your small group could take a shift serving the homeless. Intentionally strive to make your smiles, encouragement, and service a part of bringing emotional healing to these often-ostracized members of our society. Depending on your time availability, get to know some of the homeless people by listening to their stories.

God who sees
El Roi El Row.*ih*

In Genesis 16:13, the translator has supplied the word
me so that it reads "the God who sees me." More literally,
this title El Roi would be rendered *God of sight.*

FOUR

WATCHER
{GENESIS 16:1-16}

HOWARD THURMAN

*What we most want to know about God is whether He is present in the
commonplace experiences of ordinary living, available to ordinary people under
the most garden variety of circumstances.*

The floor of the concrete room is cold as she walks with a
chill to the new day. This thirteen-year-old Indonesian girl doesn't
really know where she is. Only three days ago (or was it four?), she
and a friend of hers had been drawn by curiosity from their village
to the nearby city. The sights, sounds, activities, colors, and crowds
of this bustling, third world, urban metropolis were as exciting as

she had imagined. It was a grand adventure – but this impression would soon turn to terror. As they walked along the busy street, a car sped towards the girls, then screeched to a halt right next to them. Some men the girls had never seen before suddenly grabbed the one, throwing her into the back of the car. Her screaming and kicking offered little resistance. When the car zoomed away, a blindfold prevented her from seeing where she was going, though she wouldn't have recognized her surroundings anyway.

A father sits in the dark living room, nervously wondering where his son could be. At around 2:00 a.m. he had been awakened and noticed a light shining beneath his bedroom door. Inconvenienced by his teenage son once again, he muttered a complaint about irresponsibility as he staggered into the hall to turn off the lights. Instinct told him to check the rest of the house. When he did, he discovered that his son had snuck out past curfew – again. His car was gone, and the dad had no idea where he was. Anger at his son's constant rebellion turned to concern when repeated calls to his son's cell phone were not answered. Instead of waking his wife, the dad now sits alone in the dark, wondering, fearing, praying… and crying for his son.

The parents-to-be in the doctor's office are in complete shock. Their physician's words are audible but seem muffled, and the numbness of this new reality sends the parents into an inner world of disbelief. For three years they had prayed for a child, and now they were expecting – and so grateful. Only weeks from delivery, a final ultrasound caused the doctor to order some tests. Even though the parents knew there were some concerns for the health of the baby, the continued to believe that this gift from God was going to be as perfect as they had anticipated. Within minutes, the doctor's report had shattered those hopes. The tests revealed that their unborn child had significant physical and mental limitations that would require surgery immediately upon birth. The child was not guaranteed to make it through the surgery; and even if this infant survived, the prognosis was that he would experience a short and painful life.

NO ONE'S EXEMPT

A scared little girl caught up in the sex slave industry; a father whose heart is broken, fearing for his son; parents whose joy has turned to pain. These three very dramatic, yet real, examples of life circumstances are faced in this world daily, along with millions of "lesser" struggles. This world in which we live brings many challenges great and small on several fronts. People everywhere find themselves in helpless and hopeless situations ranging from financial despair to emotional loss, from physical danger to broken relationships.

- Christians are not exempt.
- The wealthy are not exempt.
- The talented and successful are not exempt.
- Influential leaders do not get a free pass.

Sooner or later everyone, both great and small, deals with the pain of life and wonders whether or not God is aware of what is going on. *Does he really see my need?* we might be thinking. The Bible assures us that he does: "From heaven the LORD looks down and sees all mankind" (Psalm 33:13). But honestly, in life's harshest moments, sometimes it doesn't feel like it.

FEELING ALL ALONE

From the perspective of a servant girl named Hagar, it must have felt as if God was not watching. Hagar was an Egyptian handmaid caught up in the saga of Abram and Sarai (whose names God would later change to Abraham and Sarah), as recorded in the book of Genesis. Sometimes we skim over those people in the Bible who are "cast" only in supporting roles, but Hagar's circumstances highlighted in the bible narrative are worthy of our attention. In Genesis 16 we find a scared little girl in a rough situation.

- She was an outsider who had been mistreated and abandoned.
- She was a young mother who had no means to provide for her son.
- She found herself far from home and all alone.
- She was powerless to change her situation and held out little hope of deliverance.

However, in the midst of all this despair, she made a great discovery about God. In her darkest moment, she learned that God's name is El Roi, the "God who sees me" (Genesis 16:13). He is the continual, eternal Watcher... *of* all and *over* all.

Though God had promised Abram and Sarai that they would become the parents of a great nation, much time had elapsed since the Lord told Abram, "Go from your country, your people and your father's household to the land I will show you" (12:1). In spite of their obedience to God's call, they were still childless a decade later. God had reconfirmed this promise over the years, but you can't blame this man and his wife (who were well into their eighties) for becoming a little impatient.

At one point, Abram had guessed that "the one who will inherit my estate is Eliezer of Damascus." And what was his reasoning? He told God, "You have given me no children" (15:2, 3). Again, God assured Abram that he would have a son. Still, the doubts lingered. Finally in Chapter 16 of Genesis we find that Sarai decided to take matters into her own hands, which is how Hagar was drawn into the drama.

Sarai's recommendation was for Abram to take her female servant Hagar as "his wife" (16:3) and bear children through her. It is important to remember that while this idea seems incredibly inappropriate to us, according to the customs of the Eastern peoples in Abram's time, it would have been culturally acceptable. Since carrying on the family name could only be achieved by passing on one's inheritance through a male child, having a son through the wife's handmaid was a common way of ensuring this reality. Of course, God never endorsed this sort of action, but it was a practice that Sarai and Abram most likely would have witnessed in the lives of their neighbors. Hagar belonged to Sarai, and any child of Hagar's would technically belong to her master – meaning, Sarai would be credited with providing Abram a son through her servant. This is complicated thinking, but it was the way Sarai and most women of her day understood things.

In Genesis 16 we find a scared little girl in a tough situation.

The Bible reminds us, "There is a way that appears to be right, but in the end it leads to death" (Proverbs 14:12). This "Hagar as mom" plan was conceived and driven by an earthly perspective. Sarai made choices based on her human understanding and insight, but her plan lacked God's perspective on two fronts. First, she had no view to the future and how God would eventually fulfill his promise to Abram through her (which he did and he foresaw). And second, there is no indication in Scripture that God ever intended for a man to have more than one wife. Sarai surely knew that. If she'd thought about how God created marriage to be between one man and one woman from the start, she may have viewed her own situation in a different light.

Our God is a God who watches the lives of his people in their entirety – he sees the future just as clearly as he sees the past and the present.

God never intended to provide children for Abram through Hagar. His clear vision foresaw a son born to Abram and Sarai. I will concede that God did not specifically mention Sarai in his original promise to make Abram the father of many nations. It is not until we get to Genesis 17:16 that we discover that Sarai was to be the mother of this promised child. However, given God's biblical design for marriage to be experienced between one man and one woman, we can fairly deduce that he intended for Sarai to be the mother all along. (Though in Genesis 17:17 and again in Genesis 18:12, the old couple laughed at the idea.)

God was planning a miraculous birth, not a common one. The apostle Paul would later write concerning Abram's sons: "His son by the slave woman was born according to the flesh, but his son by the free woman was born as the result of a divine promise" (Galatians 4:23). God the Watcher saw clearly what was going to happen. God saw what neither Sarai or Abram could see, but the great man of faith and his wife showed little trust that God would come through.

A PLAN TO EASE THE PAIN

Abram consented to Sarai's plan and took Hagar as a wife. In no time, this young Egyptian slave girl became pregnant with Abram's child. One can only imagine the jealousy and heartache Sarai must have felt when her servant found herself in a place that Sarai had desired for many years. How many prayers had she offered – through tears – for a son? Surely the heartache intensified nine months later when a boy child was born and Abram was assured a son of inheritance – without Sarai.

Can you imagine Sarai's bitterness toward God? She was human, she had followed through on her own idea, and later she would have strong feelings as a result. Similarly, when we pursue our own ideas without seeking God's input, we feel the emotional sting and consequences of our decisions. What anticipation had filled Sarai's heart as the only wife of the one whom God had promised to make into a great nation! Now her dreams had been shattered, and Abram's heart would be inclined toward his son through Hagar. Sarai would still be his wife, but would she be relegated to second place in his affections?

It's interesting to note that Sarai ultimately blamed God for her situation. It's fair to guess that before Sarai had her Hagar idea, she wondered if God were watching. Had he not noticed that she was getting older and time was slipping away for this whole "father of many nations" thing to happen? Was her emotional pain of being childless hidden from the eyes of the Lord? Did God notice how Abram looked at her with disappointment in his eyes? Was the God of the universe unable to see the private, quiet prayer times when she was alone in the house?

One thing was clear: if God did see, he wasn't responding as Sarai had had hoped. Perhaps she concluded that God was against her. "The LORD has kept me from having children" (Genesis 16:20, she had said to her husband.

SEEING FROM A WORLDY PERSPECTIVE

When we don't view our circumstances through God's eyes, we tend to take things into our own hands. Sarai's solution to her situation was to accomplish what God had promised but hadn't delivered in the time frame that both Abram and Sarai had expected. "Go, sleep with my slave," she said. "Perhaps I can build a family through her" (16:2).

When we face life's toughest situations, our instinct is to find a human solution – and tell ourselves that God can't possibly have a better one. This often complicates things. The amazing thing is that our "impossibles" vary widely and may not even seem like a big deal to someone else. But when we experience them ourselves, they dominate our thinking and we tend to focus entirely on how we will fix the problem.

- When the doctor gives us a diagnosis of cancer, we immediately begin researching medical sites on the Internet to discover options and medical treatments concerning the disease. I have many friends and family members who, upon receiving a particular diagnosis, read everything written on the cancer in question. It feels right just to do something!

- Over the last several years as the country has faced economic challenges, it has not been uncommon for many in my church to ask for prayer because they were laid off or fired. A sudden job loss may motivate us in the same way as a health challenge. After the initial shock of the setback, it doesn't take long before one begins to update his resume and contact as many people as possible in searching for possible connections.
- The stress of a child's failing grades causes parents to meet with teachers and spend hours at the kitchen table "helping" their child make progress in his studies. (I usually ended up being more confused than my boys.)

How easy it is for us to be like Sarai. With our limited perspective, we often try to fix things on our own instead of trusting the God who sees everything.

Sarai was not the only nearsighted one in this story. Abram agreed to Sarai's solution, showing that he also shared a purely human vision of the possibilities. According to Hebrews 11:8-19 Abraham is the prototype for faithfully following God, but in this instance he lacked the great faith he is commended for. God had promised and confirmed several times that Abram would be the father of many nations. He had no reason (nor do we, scripturally) to believe that this promise did not include his wife Sarai. A child is born to a father and a mother, and since Abram was to be a father according to the promise, his wife Sarai must have been the assumed mother. But Abram consented to his wife's plan instead of trusting that God had his own plan and was watching over it all.

Listening to your spouse is not a bad idea unless the spouse is not giving godly advice. When Job was in the midst of his painful ordeal, his wife said to him, "Are you still maintaining your integrity? Curse God and die!" (Job 2:9). This is bad advice even if it *is* from your lifelong mate! No matter the relationship, advice that goes against God's plan, will, or commands will end with disastrous results. As

Christ followers today, we, like Abram, often allow ourselves to be swayed by the noisier voice, the most "common sense" voice, the voice of our true love… even when the advice goes against God's directives.

No matter the relationship, advice that goes against God's plan, will, or commands will end with disastrous results.

Recently I preached a sermon in which I listed the kinds of people we should not allow to speak into our lives. I reiterated that this was not an arrogant stance that shows an unwillingness to learn. Ultimately, we can learn something from everyone, if we pay attention. I'm talking about voices that have limited insight but that we allow to speak into our spiritual walks with a talk-show morality. Here are some of the people we should not listen to in the area of spiritual guidance.

Non-Christians, who do not see life through the lens of God's will as revealed in his Word. There is simply no way that someone who does not have faith in Jesus will give us sound biblical advice for daily living. Sarai followed the custom of giving her maidservant to her husband from the practices of the surrounding pagan nations. In essence, she listened to people who did not have God's perspective.

Of course, a non-Christian doctor can give a good headache remedy, an unbelieving dentist can pronounce a tooth rotten, a pagan mechanic can expertly replace your brakes, and an unchurched loan officer may be qualified to tell us about the latest mortgage rates. However, even in matters of their expertise, their non-Christian mind-set could steer us in the wrong direction and into actions that displease God. Take, for example, a non-Christian tax preparer whose standards may move him to fudge a little on the facts to "find" more tax refund and thus increase his profit.

Less mature Christians, who have not had enough experience with faith-shaking situations through which they stood firm and can now testify to God's continued faithfulness. This may sound a bit strange because we are talking about brothers and sisters in Christ who are filled with the Holy Spirit. Still, in the many life decisions we face, we should seek out those who have insight from a deeper level of spiritual maturity.

Cultural voices, who are blind to God's ways We are inundated every day with the voices of talk-show hosts, news commentators, celebrity bloggers, and media pundits – and if we are not careful, we will allow these voices to be the main influence in our thinking and actions. Just think how much moral ground we have lost from the time Elvis Presley could not be shown on TV from the waist down because of his sexually suggestive gyrations. Our current media culture has progressively added more blurs and bleeps – and sometimes doesn't even bother to add blurs and bleeps! Jesus warned, "If the blind lead the blind, both will fall into a pit" (Matthew 15:14).

God is not only watching our current situation; he clearly sees our future as well. His watching is perfect, and we must be tuned in to him. When we forget that God has long-term vision, we often listen to the advice of others instead of following God. If we think God is oblivious to the entirety of our situation, that he does not see our desired outcome, or that he isn't complying with our instant-gratification timing, we may be inclined to listen to lesser voices. Sarai gave bad advice to Abram because she did not have God's watching ability in mind. Because no one in our lives has full understanding of God's watchful eye, we must listen to voices that will encourage us to trust God's vision even when the outcome can't be seen. Sarai should have encouraged Abram to keep trusting because she trusted that God was watching over their situation and knew the outcome. When she didn't give this advice, Abram should have realized her frustration and reminded her of God's providence and guidance.

> **When we forget that God has long-term vision, we often listen to the advice of others instead of following God.**

When we try to fix our situation on our own – particularly when our actions are opposed to what we already know God wants – or listen to and act on someone's unwise advice, things usually go from bad to worse. That's exactly what happened next in the Genesis 16 narrative.

Sarai blamed Abram ("You are responsible for the wrong I am suffering") and mistreated Hagar (16:5, 6). There is no way of knowing what Sarai had expected, emotionally, when she suggested that Abram sleep with her servant. There is no indication that she thought about how she might react if her plan really did work and Hagar became pregnant. Scripture doesn't give us those details.

And… what was Abram thinking? Did he think that this "extra wife relationship" wouldn't somehow come between him and Sarai? At the very lowest moral thinking, maybe lust was the motivation for Abram's agreeing. At the very best, he was hoping that perhaps God was going to begin fulfilling his promise by giving him a son through Hagar. Either way, at some point he must have reasoned that this was the best thing to do.

Both Abram and Sarai were terribly nearsighted. As a result, Hagar's life – as well as their own lives – became painful. Similarly, when we act without considering our God who sees it all, others often get hurt and we do too.

ON THE RUN

Hagar did indeed get pregnant, and her attitude toward Sarai changed. "She began to despise her mistress" (16:4). In turn Sarai complained to Abram and began to treat Hagar harshly. Perhaps she increased Hagar's workload. Maybe she made disparaging comments or yelled at her. It could be that Sarai punished her physically for any mistakes she made. We don't know; the Bible only tells us that "Sarai mistreated Hagar; so she fled from her" (v. 6). In distress, Hagar fled to the desert of loneliness, fearing for her safety, and running next to who-knows-where. Even the angel of the LORD asked her, "Where are you going?" (v. 8). If our tendency isn't to fix our situations in our own wisdom like Sarai, it is often to run from our trouble like Hagar.

- When marriage becomes a challenge, we may forget that God sees the emotional toll of harsh words, hastily spoken.
- When good health seems elusive, it feels as though God does not see our pain.
- When we fail, we may not sense his present and watchful eye in our disappointment.
- When we are alone, we stare into space looking for his loving gaze of companionship.

When we, like Hagar sit alone and tired on the desert road of running away, it is good to be reminded that our God's name is Watcher. David wrote about El Roi's range of vision in one of his songs. Psalm 139 is a tribute to God's awareness of our total being.

- "You know when I sit and when I rise" (Psalm 139:2). God always knows what we are doing.
- "You perceive my thoughts from afar" (v. 2). God always knows what we are thinking.
- "Before a word is on my tongue you, LORD, know it completely" (v. 4). God always knows what we're going to say.
- God is everywhere we go, no matter where we go (see vv. 7-10).
- "You knit me together in my mother's womb" (v. 13). God knew us before we were born.
- "All the days ordained for me were written in your book before one of them came to be" (v. 16). God knows the stages and length of our lives.
- "Search me, God, and know my heart; test me and know my anxious thoughts" (v. 23). God sees our hearts and our worries.

What was true for David was true for Hagar as well. As she sat by a spring in the desert, God was saying to her, "I see you, Hagar." A dialogue ensued between Hagar and the angel whom God had sent – helping her discover God in a whole new way. Maybe she thought that she was too insignificant for God to notice. Maybe she assumed that God couldn't be bothered with watching a lowly servant girl. Maybe she thought that God saw her as an Egyptian foreigner, as her mistress did. If so, she thought wrong on all counts.

Perhaps you too feel as though God doesn't have time to watch over you, look at your life, see your pain, and envision your future. If so, you would be underestimating God. When Hagar became aware that God was watching, she called him El Roi. Genesis 16:13 says, "She gave this name to the LORD who spoke to her: 'You are the God who sees me,' for she said, 'I have now seen the One who sees me.'" Discovering God's watching changed everything for Hagar.

NEVER OUT OF HIS SIGHT

When we understand that we're always under God's watchful eye, life seems less scary. When my oldest son, Mikey, was three (we still call him Mikey, though he is in his mid-twenties), we were involved in a youth ministry near Orlando, Florida. We spent some great days as a family, going to the beach and soaking up the sun. We played in the surf, built sand castles, ate at a local restaurant, and applied gallons of sunscreen.

The beach can be a challenging place for parents, as they must constantly keep their children in view. And Mikey was always very independent. One particular day as I watched from my lounge chair on the beach, he began to wander down the shoreline. He was distracted by sand crabs, seashells, and the squishy freedom of the temperate surf between his toes. Instead of instructing him to come closer to our location (i.e., yelling "Hey, get back over here!"), I simply began to follow him from a distance.

Completely unaware of any potential danger in his surroundings, and caught up in his grand adventure, he walked for nearly a mile before acknowledging my presence. I had watched his every move from afar, ready to respond if he called and willing to rush to his side if he needed help.

At some point, he looked up, turned his head, and said, "Dad, come look at this." He couldn't have known that I was there, but he trusted, took it for granted, that his father would be nearby.

As we made our way back up the beach to his mom and his younger brother, I thought about how God must watch over us in the same way. Our circumstances may cause us to wander all over this beach called life, but we are never truly lost, because he is always watching over us. We are never out of his sight and never beyond a point where we can call his name. He is El Roi, the God who watches over all of us.

Hagar returned to her mistress without any change of circumstance. The angel of God had commanded her: "Go back to your mistress and submit to her" (16:9). It was necessary for Hagar to apologize and accept any punishment Sarai deemed appropriate. She still needed to perform the duties of a servant as before. The uncomfortable feeling of jealousy would likely remain between Sarai and her. Hagar would have to guard her demeanor around her mistress. She would always be linked with Abram as the father of her child, but any notion of gaining the rights of a wife was unrealistic. Hagar and her son would remain in Abram's house as strangers from a foreign land. Sarai might still decide to mistreat her.

Perhaps you too feel as though God doesn't have time to watch over you, look at your life, see your pain and envision your future.

Even though all the circumstances that caused Hagar to flee still remained, Hagar returned because she knew that none of it was hidden from God's sight. He would see her in every situation, and his presence would mean everything.

GAINING INSIGHT

There are three short lessons as we consider what El Roi means to us:

Don't run ahead of God. Since God is watching over you, you can trust him to help you through any problem or challenge you may face. If Sarai had simply waited on God and trusted his timing, she would have become the mother of Abram's firstborn and this painful episode would have been avoided. In times of trouble, turn to God first and wait on him to move.

Don't run from your situation. You can be sure that God is aware of your circumstances. Whatever situation you may find yourself in, God sees you where you are. God saw Hagar being mistreated and resting by a spring in the desert, and you can trust that he is aware of you as well. Often, when we feel that God is unaware of harsh conditions, words spoken against us, or pain that we are experiencing, he is most present – watching over us while also guiding, providing, and comforting as we grow through it all.

Don't worry about what the future holds. God sees that too. Hagar was worried about her future, but God even had his eyes on her *son's* future. He told her that she would have a son, that his name would be Ishmael, and that he would live as a wild man against everyone (vv. 11, 12). Though this final promise may not have been the most welcome of blessings, it assured Hagar that God was watching out for her future. She took comfort in this watchful care. In fact, a few chapters later, God rescued Hagar and her son by providing water in the desert when she thought death was imminent (21:15-21). We can trust that God sees our future and will act in love with our best interests in mind.

This chapter opened with a scared girl, an anxious father, and shocked parents-to-be. Did they know that the God who sees was watching over them? It would make all the difference.

FIRST-NAME BASIS
For individual or group study

1. Have you (or someone close to you) ever experienced the disappointment of infertility? What emotions seem to be the strongest for the would-be mothers in this situation?

2. Using vision as a metaphor, classify how you see your future. Is your vision 20/20, out of focus, nearsighted, farsighted, or blind?

3. In the Genesis 16 narrative, who do you most relate to: Sarai, Abram, or Hagar? Why?

4. What difficult situation are you in the middle of right now? In what specific ways has God revealed to you that he is aware of your situation (assuming an angel hasn't appeared to you on the side of the road)?

5. What is going on in this world right now that you find hard to believe that God is watching? Why? What do you think God might be doing in that situation, even though you can't see it? What do you think God *should* be doing? What Scriptures do you base your idea on?

GETTING ACQUAINTED WITH
EL ROI

1. Look again at page 71, where we noted from Psalm 139 seven things that El Roi sees in our lives. Write these seven on a sheet of paper; then personalize at least three of them by identifying your reality in each statement. Spend some time contemplating each and thanking God for his perfect vision of everything about you.

2. Find an hour in your schedule and a quiet place (to serve as your spring in the desert) to speak frankly with God about an area of your life in which it feels like God doesn't see your

circumstance. Write the situation down. Then spend the entire hour speaking to God of this concern and listening for his still, small voice. As you do so, meditate on these Scriptures: Psalms 1:6; 63:6; 121:1-8. Thank God for seeing your circumstance even when you've felt as if he didn't.

3. Make a list of the things in your life that you wish God *didn't* see. (You can do this mentally if you are uncomfortable writing them down.) Then find an hour in a quiet place to invite God's spirit to guide you as you ask the following questions concerning your list:

- Why do I wish God couldn't see these things?
- What does El Roi's seeing these things mean about our relationship?
- What does El Roi's seeing these things mean about his love for me?
- What might God see in the future concerning these things?

Conclude this time of reflection by declaring to God that you know he sees things about you that you wish he didn't. Ask him to help you overcome those things you wish were not issues in your life, and say that you look forward to the day when they will be distant memories.

Lord of Armies
Jehovah Sabaoth Jeh.*ho*. vuh Tshe.bah.*oat*

Variations of this name are used throughout the Old Testament:
Elohim Sabaoth (God of armies) and Jehovah Elohim Sabaoth (Lord
God of armies). Older translations render the word *sabaoth* as *hosts*
rather than *armies*. Sometimes this name signifies that God is in
charge of heavenly armies; other times, it means armies of men.

FIVE

PROTECTOR
{1 SAMUEL 1:3; 2 KINGS 6:8-23; PSALM 80:4}

A. W. Tozer

*We are on safe ground only when we know what kind of God He is and adjust
our entire being to the holy concept.*

The man's hands are shaking. He has key testimony against the
leader of a crime organization, a powerful organization. Testifying
could put his own life in danger. What to do? Thankfully, help
is available. He can enter what we commonly call the Witness
Protection Program (officially called the Witness Security Program).
The promise of protection has given thousands of informants the

courage to take the witness stand in court. According to the U.S. Marshals website, "The U.S. Marshals have protected, relocated and given new identities to more than 8,300 witnesses and 9,800 of their family members, since the program began in 1971."[18] Though their testimony posed a real threat to their lives and the lives of their families, such witnesses were assured that the U.S. Marshals Service would keep them safe. According to this government agency's records, no witness who has come under their protection and followed their protocol has ever been harmed!

Such security is possible only if the force protecting the witnesses is mightier than those who would harm them. The way to overcome a dangerous foe is to counter with superior protection. This is true in the world of government protection and in the spiritual battle for the souls of mankind.

THE COMMANDER IN CHIEF AND HIS ARMY

In the Old Testament the Hebrew word *tsaba* is used to describe the powerful, protecting force of an army. This word is used more than 450 times in the Jewish Scriptures (according to the *KJV* count) and is most commonly translated into the English word *army*.[19] The word literally means "that which goes forth" (as in an army going forth in battle). This word is also used to describe a large number of things other than soldiers. In Genesis 2:1 it describes the totality of the entire universe of creation ("all their vast array"). Scripture also uses this word to describe the hosts of Heaven (Psalm 148:2), a large army of angels mobilized for God's purpose. The word carries the idea of an advancing multitude of overwhelming power. In the days when kings advanced to conquer other territories, as we find in the Old Testament record, an approaching army was one of the most awe-inspiring images a person could evoke. It meant either the terror of impending defeat or the celebration of protection.

This word for *army* expands to the Hebrew word *tsebaoth*

(usually rendered *sabaoth* in English letters) and combines with God's personal name as Jehovah Elohim Sabaoth to describe a God of force and power. This name is sometimes translated as *Lord God Almighty*. Because God is in charge of all the hosts of creation, he is Protector of his people. He commands all the entities in the universe, all the stars, and all the angelic hosts. There is no army bigger or stronger than the army of the Lord. Jehovah Sabaoth is the only real Protector we can rely on.

GOD'S POWERFUL PROTECTION PLAN

We'll look at two biblical narratives that introduce us to God as commander of a considerable army. The first is found in 1 Samuel 1:3: "Year after year [Elkanah] went up from his town to worship and sacrifice to the LORD Almighty at Shiloh." We can conjecture that when Samuel wrote this book, he was making a statement about his God by calling him Jehovah Sabaoth ("LORD Almighty") in the first three verses of his story. The historical period in which Samuel wrote followed about three hundred years during which the people of Israel were led by judges. Because God's people had rebelled, he frequently punished them by allowing the surrounding nations (especially the Philistines) to oppress them with military might. From time to time God raised up leaders (judges like Ehud, Deborah, Gideon, Samson, and Jehu) to lead against these foreign foes, with armies they had mustered with God's help.

When the book of Samuel begins, the people were well aware of armies, having been both subdued and protected by these forces throughout the years. They found themselves tenuously positioned close to Philistine territory, with the place of worship and the ark of the covenant located in Shiloh.

The way to overcome a dangerous foe is to counter with superior protection.

In short order the ark was captured by the Philistine army (1 Samuel 4:17). Eli the high priest must have been shocked enough when he heard that his sons Hophni and Phinehas had been killed in battle; but when he heard that the ark of God had been captured, he fell backward off his chair, causing him to die of a broken neck. Eli's daughter-in-law was pregnant with Phinehas's child at the time. When she became aware of all the news, she went into labor and gave birth. Overcome by labor pains, as she was dying she named her son Ichabod, meaning "no glory," which highlighted this dark day as the day "the Glory has departed from Israel" (v. 21). The prophet Samuel had begun his book of history by reminding the people that God was their Protector by name – "LORD Almighty," Lord of all armies (1:3). This is a truth they would need to hang onto.

Another place in which we discover God as Protector is found in the Jewish hymnbook knows as Psalms. The songwriter Asaph composed a song in which he begged the Lord for deliverance from his people's captors: "How long, LORD God Almighty, will your anger smolder against the prayers of your people?" (Psalm 80:4). We can't be sure exactly what conflict Asaph was referencing, but many think "this may well represent the eighth century [BC] Assyrian crisis."[20] If so, the psalm was written with full knowledge of the powerful Assyrian army just north of Israel's territory – making the reference to his name Jehovah Elohim Sabaoth very significant indeed! All who sang this song were acknowledging God's power to protect them from advancing armies with a superior army of his own.

These two Scriptures give us just a glimpse of the protection afforded God's people throughout their history. Additionally:

- When God's people were trapped between the Red Sea to the east and Pharaoh's advancing army from the west, Jehovah Sabaoth's pillar of cloud moved to protect them (Exodus 14:19, 20).

- When Daniel was wrongly condemned to the lions' den, Jehovah Sabaoth "sent his angel, and he shut the mouths of the lions" (Daniel 6:22) to protect his servant.
- When Joshua was preparing to lead the army of Israel into the promised land on a military campaign, the commander of the army of the Lord appeared to him, a reminder of God's presence and protection over Joshua's initiatives (Joshua 5:13-15).

How did Jehovah Sabaoth actually fight these battles on behalf of his people? A story from the life of the prophet Elisha gives us some insight.

THWARTING THE ENEMY'S PLANS

The story of 2 Kings 6 appropriately begins with a king advancing with a powerful army. When we catch up with the king of the northern region called Aram, he is in attack mode against Israel. In high-level strategic planning sessions with his commanders, this king was setting up camps from which he could ambush the Israelite army.

But he was repeatedly unsuccessful. It seems the prophet Elisha was sabotaging these plans by warning the king of Israel of the enemy's exact locations: "Beware of passing that place, because the Arameans are going down there" (2 Kings 6:9). Time and time again, the king of Israel used this information to avoid attacks from the king of Aram.

Finally, this pagan king got tired of his secret plans being revealed, and he convened a meeting of his officers. His suspicion was that one of them was a spy. He demanded, "Tell me! Which of us is on the side of the king of Israel?" (v. 11). The answer he was given was that the Israelite Elisha was invading his most private moments through his prophetic gift. This changed the king of Aram's entire tactical approach to conquering the Israelites. If the king of Aram could simply take out this meddling prophet, he would be able to continue his secret plans against his enemy. When the king of Aram discovered Elisha was living in Dothan, "he sent horses and chariots and a strong force there. They went by night and surrounded the city" (v. 14).

Imagine Elisha's servant waking up the next day to begin his daily chores (it must have been tough working for a guy who had insight into everything that happened!), only to find that this small city was surrounded by an army. Obviously shaken, he hurried back into the house of his master and told him the alarming news. I wonder if it ever crossed his mind that his boss, being a prophet, already knew that the army was there. After all, it was Elisha who had informed the king of Israel of every move the enemy had previously made. The servant nervously communicated that there was a considerable army waiting outside. He wondered aloud how they might get out of this precarious position, crying, "Oh no, my lord! What shall we do?" (v. 15).

NOT UNAWARE

It was a great question for Elisha, and it's a great question for us as well. When evil forces have hemmed us in on every side, what are we to do? Too often the problem is that we don't even realize there *is* an enemy like this king of Aram launching attacks against us on every front. It is unlikely that you have a real, physical army assembled against you (though it's possible). Aside from an occasional run-in with an irate driver, an angry coworker, an aggressive neighbor, or a playground bully, most of us rarely face deadly physical threats. However, the Bible is clear that there is certainly a spiritual foe that we should pay attention to.

As my good friend, Dr. J. K. Jones, has pointed out, "any Christian who strives for personal holiness is in for the fight of their life." We need our Protector because there is a cosmic spiritual war going on. Just consider these "glimpses of war" (Jones) that we find in Scripture.

- "The prince of this world will be driven out" (John 12:31).
- Jesus prays, "Protect them from the evil one" (17:15).
- "Satan himself masquerades as an angel of light" (2 Corinthians 11:14).
- "Do not give the devil a foothold" (Ephesians 4:27).
- "Take your stand against the devil's schemes... Our struggle is... against the powers of this dark world and against the spiritual forces of evil" (6:11, 12).
- "By his death he might break the power of him who holds the power of death – that is, the devil" (Hebrews 2:14).
- "Your enemy the devil prowls around like a roaring lion" (1 Peter 5:8).
- "Then war broke out in heaven" (Revelation 12:7).

Clearly, if we align ourselves with Jesus Christ, we are thrust into the eternal power struggle between good and evil, right and wrong, God and Satan. Satan's doom and our victory have been sealed through Jesus' death, burial, and resurrection; but the devil fights on in spite of this.

Providentially, as the king of Israel had insight through God's prophet, we have insight through the Scriptures into the positions from which Satan attacks us. As the apostle Paul says, "We are not unaware of his schemes" (2 Corinthians 2:11). There is a heavenly and spiritual war going on, but it is being fought on earthly battlefields that are clearly marked out as we strive to follow Jesus. The apostle Peter admonished us "to abstain from sinful desires, which wage war against your soul" (1 Peter 2:11).

Satan's doom and our victory have been sealed through Jesus' death, burial, and resurrection; but the devil fights on in spite of this.

Exactly what are these schemes and desires? The apostle John clearly marked the spiritual battlefields we face on three fronts: "Everything in the world – the lust of the flesh, the lust of the eyes, and the pride of life – comes not from the Father but from the world" (1 John 2:16).

The lust of the flesh

The war against Satan takes place on the battlefield of our flesh. We live in bodies that are prone to sin. Originally we were created perfectly with five senses to enjoy God's blessings. I'll mention four of the senses here and give more detailed insight into the fifth in a moment.

- We were created with a sense of taste, through which we can sample a wide range of foods like strawberries and french fries.
- Our noses were designed to let us experience an incredible variety of fragrances like roses and fresh-baked bread.
- Our skin was designed to feel everything we touch – from hot and cold water to soft baby skin and rough sandpaper.
- We were also created to enjoy the numerous sounds that fill our existence – from the hovering buzz of a hummingbird's wings to the soothing notes of a harpist's strings.
- Unfortunately, these senses that let us enjoy the good things God has given us can also be used by Satan to become sin. Eating can be a sacred fellowship (as in the Lord's Supper), or it can be abused through gluttony (can you say Chinese buffet?). Drinks can be refreshing, but drinking alcohol in excess can have devastating results. Sex can be a beautiful union of touch between husband and wife, but it can also be a selfish act outside the context of marriage and completely devoid of love. We can expose our ears to words of encouragement and praise, or we can listen to communication that deeply injures someone (see James 3:9, 10).

The lust of the eyes

I intentionally omitted sight from the list of senses above. What we *see* seems to represent a place of struggle in this spiritual war that deserves its own category. Our eyes are equipped to view every color in the spectrum displayed in countless ways on the canvas of God's creation, but they are also the place where sin is often conceived. Jesus said, "The eye is the lamp of the body" (Matthew 6:22). Whatever we see gets inside us and lights our hearts. Our eyes are able to mentally photograph God's awesome creation (even as I type, the view from my plane window affords a remarkable sunset over a huge bank of storm clouds), but they can also cause us to worship and serve "created things rather than the Creator" (Romans 1:25). To lust is to deeply desire the beautiful things God has surrounded us with more than we desire God. The lust of the eyes leads us to selfishly want what we observe, for our own glory and pleasure.

The pride of life

Finally, the war against Satan takes place on the battlefield of pride. When our focus in life becomes how we can please ourselves through the senses that God has given us, we are essentially removing God from the throne of our hearts and replacing him with our own desires. We elevate ourselves as better than God, which in turn leads to our thinking more highly of ourselves than those around us. Pride can be so subtle that we often miss it, but it is lived out in our world in a variety of ways.

- A star athlete may become unhappy because though his team won, his efforts weren't the deciding factor and he didn't receive the accolades.
- A businessperson might become jealous of a coworker who receives the promotion she had hoped for.

- A band member might go out of his way to let everyone know that he is the creative genius behind the music or the most talented in the band.
- A housewife whose diet and exercise have given her a fresh body image may be tempted to spend hours in the gym until it becomes an obsession.
- Even in church, a pastor or ministry leader can desire the praises of men more than the blessing God, so he must be on guard against an unhealthy and inflated ego.

The battleground of pride is a real threat to our spiritual well-being. In an instant, Satan can twist an overstated compliment meant to encourage, a consistent pattern of success at work, or a glance in the mirror on a good hair day to deceive us into believing that we are somebody special. Before you know it, we are not relying on God the Protector but in our own imagined greatness.

WHAT SHALL WE DO?

It is on those same three battlegrounds that the very first spiritual battle for souls on earth took place. Satan fought with the first man and woman in human history, and he hasn't changed his war plan since then. Satan appeared to Eve in Genesis 3. Satan appealed to the flesh by convincing Eve that fruit from the forbidden tree was "good for food" and "desirable for gaining wisdom" (3:6). The tree was also "pleasing to the eye" (v. 6), and Satan used that beauty to distract from God's command. Finally, the serpent appealed to Eve's pride by planting in her heart a desire to "be like God" (v. 5).

Today we need the Protector's help to defeat our enemy as he employs these tried-and-true tactics against us. In many ways we find ourselves as helpless and powerless as Elisha's servant must have felt.

Back at Dothan, Elisha's servant was in the middle of a clearly marked battlefield that he hadn't bargained for. He had no idea how he, his master Elisha, or the people of that city could possibly defend themselves against the large and powerful army surrounding them. There seemed to be no possible way for them to escape or overcome their opponent.

Elisha, on the other hand, remained completely calm. He told his servant not to be afraid, because he knew it wasn't about "What shall we do?" but about "those who are with us" (2 Kings 6:16). In fact, Elisha could see that the Lord of armies, Jehovah Sabaoth, had assembled *his* army in the hills surrounding the city; and Elisha prayed for his servant to be able to see the same: "Open his eyes, LORD, so that he may see" (v. 17).

The Lord answered this prayer by giving the servant a glimpse into the spiritual realm. Now, instead of seeing an Aramean army with chariots, horses, swords, and spears, his attention was averted to the hills surrounding the city; and there he saw another army. He "saw the hills full of horses and chariots of fire all around Elisha" (v. 17).

We can be sure that this was the army of the Lord and that the Protector was coming to the defense of his people and his prophet in a miraculous way. At that powerful moment of truth, when the servant became aware of these spiritual forces that we on his side, he found courage.

In reality, his situation remained very much the same. The determined king of Aram was still bent on destroying the prophet. An enemy army still surrounded the city, preventing any efforts to escape. There was still a real enemy, and a real battle was imminent. But the discovery of Jehovah Sabaoth's presence in the servant's real-world battle made the difference for him.

Nearly twenty-five years ago, a healthy baby girl was born to a mom who had suffered brain damage and had been diagnosed with schizophrenia. Baby Sabrina was likely the product of a one-night stand, and as a result never got to meet her father. Immediately after her birth, the state took custody of the newborn and placed her in a foster home. At just the same time, a young Christian couple – even though they already had three children of their own – felt God leading them to register as foster parents.

Eight months into Sabrina's life, a devastating house fire destroyed her home. She was literally passed through the window of the house to safety as flames and smoke billowed around her young frame. As officials scrambled to place the now-homeless orphan, they called Rick and Kathy, the couple who had been praying for God to give them a child. Within hours, Sabrina, still smelling of smoke, clutched her new mom – and wouldn't let go. Not long after the fire, Rick and Kathy adopted Sabrina. She was raised to be a follower of Christ, and she currently serves on a church staff as a worship leader. God the protector had an awesome plan for this infant – though she knew nothing of what was happening around her.

Elisha's prayer impacted his servant. And Rick and Kathy's prayer – for a child they didn't even know yet – impacted Sabrina's life. We can find courage for the conflicts in our lives because we know that the God of all the armies is our defense against even the most dangerous of foes. He has no shortage of weapons... and neither do we.

EQUIPPED FOR BATTLE

In his letter to the church at Ephesus, the apostle Paul spent considerable time reminding us that God has given us, the members of his army, all we need for our defense. We must put on this armor so that we can take our "stand against the devil's schemes" (Ephesians 6:11). Paul used this word *stand* four times in verses 11-14, indicating this armor is for defense against Satan's attacks. Jehovah Sabaoth is the God who protects us, but part of his plan is to equip us for the battle and the enemy we face. Though God has done all the work through Jesus, Ephesians 6:10-18 itemizes the armor that has been provided in order to battle the enemy successfully. Christians are encouraged by the Protector's strong defense, and we are armed for battle through his Holy Spirit living in us. The Protector has equipped his followers with these weapons of protection:

- **Belt of truth** – Stand with the "belt of truth buckled around your waist" (Ephesians 6:14). God's truth binds each person's life together like a belt cinched tight to hold a soldier's armor in place. Truth protects us from a world filled with the devil's lies about money, sexuality, self-worth, and purpose.
- **Breastplate of righteousness** – Keep "the breastplate of righteousness in place" (v. 14). Through God's help, living a right life (living God's way) protects our hearts as a soldier's breastplate protected his. Righteousness protects us from the devil's temptation to live evil lives of greed, prejudice, and malice.
- **Shoes of peace** – Your feet are "fitted with the readiness that comes from the gospel of peace" (v. 15). Sure footing in our walk with God is provided through the peace of knowing that God is present in our lives. Peace protects us from despair when we face the hardships of life like cancer, injury, broken relationships, addictions, and death of loved ones.
- **Shield of faith** – "Take up the shield of faith" (v. 16). A Roman soldier's shield deflected weapons being hurled at him, and our main defense against Satan's arrows is faith. The devil repeatedly reminds us of the "unfair" circumstances of life, the "unanswered" prayers, and sometimes the "unhappy" life of sacrifice for Jesus. Faith – like Elisha's servant's understanding that God's army was in the hills – protects us from the dangers we see because of our trust that the Lord of all the armies is near.

> **Truth protects us from a world filled with the devil's lies about money, sexuality, self-worth, and purpose.**

- **Helmet of salvation** – Wear "the helmet of salvation" (v. 17). One strong blow to the head in battle could prove fatal to a soldier. Our understanding that we are saved by faith in Jesus Christ protects our minds from doubt. The devil seeks to shake our faith by causing us to question our worthiness or by placing doubts about our standing as one of God's children. The helmet of salvation protects us by reminding us of the saving grace of Jesus.

- **Sword of the Spirit** – Rely on "the sword of the Spirit" (v. 17). Though we are standing our ground, there is still use for the sword, an offensive weapon to defend the advances of Satan. Just as Jesus countered the devil's temptations in the desert with the Word of God (see Matthew 4:1-11), we too are protected through knowing the Word of God. In the heat of battle, when the devil attacks we find spiritual protection in the pages of the Scriptures by reading or recalling what we know to be true.

- **Prayer** – "Pray in the Spirit on all occasions" (Ephesians 6:18). Though Paul did not assign prayer as a specific piece of armor, it is the most powerful, all-encompassing defense we have against Satan. Praying protects us by giving us direct access to Jehovah Sabaoth. When we pray we have the ear of the one who commands all the armies of the universe. In fact, it was through prayer that Elisha engaged the army of God to defeat the Aramean army.

A MIGHTY TRIUMPH

Elisha was fully aware of the heavenly army that the enemy couldn't see. As the king of Aram advanced, Elisha prayed for the Lord to strike his enemies with blindness. We are not given details about the struggles in the spiritual realm here, but we can imagine the chariots and horses of fire in God's army rushing swiftly into the ranks of the army of demons who were directing the Arameans. As angels and demons clashed in cosmic battle, the physical result was that the entire army of the king of Aram was blinded. If we could see into the spiritual realm, we would have seen a battleground littered with demonic defeat. The Lord's hosts had won a mighty victory!

Now that the entire army was blinded, Elisha himself went to meet them. He told them, "This is not the road and this is not the city. Follow me, and I will lead you to the man you are looking for" (2 Kings 6:19). Then he led them to Samaria. Samaria was the capital city of the northern kingdom of Israel, so not only did Jehovah Sabaoth protect Elisha from this foreign king; he also delivered this army into the hands of his people. When the captured army entered the city gates, Elisha prayed for their eyes to be opened, and they realized they had been taken captive. Instead of killing the Arameans as the king of Israel suggested, Elisha ordered that they be fed. They were served "a great feast" (v. 3) and sent on their way.

This resulted in the protection of Jehovah Sabaoth for his people, moving forward. Apparently, the conquering king of Aram had had enough of this meddling prophet and his powerful God. He must have realized that he could not defeat a people whose God constantly came to their defense. The Scripture simply says, "So the bands from Aram stopped raiding Israel's territory" (v. 23).

PROTECTED FOR ETERNITY

Though Israel found protection from God in this instance, there certainly were more kings and other armies who would advance against the people of God in the future. This is the nature of physical war, and it is the nature of the spiritual battle we face daily as we follow Christ. It should also be noted that when we stray from following and trusting God as our Protector, he sometimes allows us to face the battle alone. These defeats are meant to turn our hearts back to him as our only true Protector. The book of Isaiah documents well how God used defeat in war to draw his people back to him. He longed for their repentance so that he could protect them once again.

We are reminded in Scripture of our need to depend on him: "for our struggle is not against flesh and blood, but against the rulers, against the authorities, against the powers of this dark world and against the spiritual forces of evil in the heavenly realms" (Ephesians 6:12). We sometimes forget that Satan will come against us time and time again in a variety of ways. One of the most compelling verses in the bible comes after the devil had tempted Jesus and lost. Satan "left him until an opportune time" (Luke 4:13).

Satan would be back. Jesus faced more spiritual battles right up to the cross – and even being mocked and challenged to come down from the cross and save himself. Those taunting words were spoken by men, but Satan's army was behind them. Thankfully, Jesus remained on the cross and came to our defense in the most incredible way. For our protection, he overcame both death and sin by his blood, death, burial, and resurrection. We may find ourselves in a daily battle for our souls, but we are safe because Jehovah Sabaoth not only commands the army; he gave his Son's life in battle so that we might be saved.

Thousands in America have found protection in the government's Witness Protection Program, and in Christ we also have security. Our identities have been changed into the image of our Savior, and as we bear witness to his name, we are protected from any harm. Though many of Christ's witnesses throughout the church's history suffered pain and even physical death, they have security in God the Protector because the force protecting the witnesses is mightier than those who would harm them.

FIRST-NAME BASIS
For individual or group study

1. What physical war in your lifetime is the most memorable? What impact has it made on your life?
2. When have you felt surrounded and overwhelmed by intimidating circumstances, as Elisha's servant was? What emotion did you feel the strongest at that time?
3. Read Ephesians 6:10-20. When have you sensed the protection of one or more of these pieces of armor in your spiritual life? How did the Protector deliver you in this instance?
4. Of the weapons and armor mentioned in Ephesians 6, which do you resonate with the most? Why? Which item do you need more practice "putting on"? What one action step can you take in that direction?
5. Which of the following descriptions best matches your spiritual stance at the present time?

   _____ stumbling
   _____ wobbly
   _____ sure-footed
   _____ rock solid
   _____ other: _____

   Why did you choose the description you did?

GETTING ACQUAINTED WITH
JEHOVAH SABAOTH

1. Across the top of a sheet of paper, write the five senses as the heads of five columns. Use this paper as a journal for the next twenty-four hours to record all that you experience in your flesh. For example, under *taste*, you might write

"chocolate chip cookies"; under *touch,* "cold wind on my face"; and under *smell,* "freshly mowed grass." Note the experiences you have with your senses until you have ten or twelve items for each of the five senses.

Did you discover any battlegrounds? Which of your senses seem to be more prone to danger in the spiritual battle? Ask the Protector to help defend you on that battleground.

2. Employ the sword of the Spirit that the Protector has provided for your defense. First, identify a spiritual battleground or spiritual foe that you are facing right now (i.e., what forces of Satan seem to have you surrounded?). Next, using a Bible concordance, look up any word you can think of that relates to your battleground. (For example, if your battleground happens to be your mouth, look up words like *mouth, tongue, lips, speech* and *words.*) Next, write down any bible verse that speaks to your specific struggle. Finally read the Scriptures you have recorded – several times. Work on committing one or several of them to memory so that you'll be armed for battle the next time temptation arises.

SIX

GUIDE
{PSALM 27:1; EXODUS 13:17-22}

Joseph M. Stowell

Biblical truth is the filter through which all information, deliberation, and decisions must be processed. Only God's truth can accurately and authoritatively reject false values and distinguish that which is true.

A good guide makes all the difference. My wife and I found this to be true on a trip we took with some good friends to our nation's capital. Our simple plan (actually, there was no plan) was to experience Washington, D.C., and the surrounding historical places at a leisurely pace in one week.

Each morning began with the most crucial decision: where would we eat breakfast. Being the Internet researcher and food aficionado that my wife is, she discovered a historic restaurant near the White House called Old Ebbitt Grill. Apparently, this place had been frequented by all kinds of civil servants, military leaders, and elected government officials throughout its history and continues to attract the important crowd in Washington. Oh, and the information said the food was good too!

On the day we were planning on dining at this legendary eatery, we parked and followed the directions we had been given, but after fifteen minutes we determined the directions were faulty. I wanted to keep wandering around until we happened upon the place (my natural male instinct… and the way Columbus discovered America, by the way), but the wives insisted on asking for help.

When our friend Lisa asked a local on the street for directions, we not only received guidance for breakfast but also an opportunity for a guided tour of the White House.

As it turned out, this friendly lady had a significant role in our government's Office of Management and Budget (OMB) and enough authority to get us an unscheduled visit. She gave us a phone number and said that if we'd call in about an hour, she would be able to get us into our nation's most important home that day!

Later that morning we arrived at the agreed-upon location and met a young history student who was doing an internship with the government's OMB. We found her to be very friendly and knowledgeable as we engaged her in conversation on the short walk to the White House. We walked to the security checkpoint, stated our names, and showed our photo IDs; then the four of us followed our guide right into the residence of the president of the United States.

It was here that I realized the importance of a guided tour. Frankly, I'm usually the independent type who likes to explore on my own, but on this occasion, even I could see the advantage of following someone who had been there before. Our guide helped us in several ways:

- Immediately, our guide began to lead us from room to room, navigating past the larger crowds of twenty to thirty tourists.
- She also directed us to the best locations for each point of interest.

- Many of the rooms we entered looked familiar to me because I had seen them in some historic photo or a news clip, but our guide gave us background information that made them come alive.
- When we had specific questions, she took time to answer them in detail.
- When we wanted to see something specific, she promised to lead us there.
- When we needed to strategically avoid the crowd to get the best view of something, she showed us a shortcut.

Seeing the White House is cool, but having a personal guide who knows where she's going and what she's talking about makes the experience so much richer. If a guide is necessary for a greater experience at 1600 Pennsylvania Avenue, then a guide is certainly needed for our journey through life. As we will discover in this chapter, there is no Guide like God.

THE LIGHT

Our God is known by a name that signifies his guidance in our lives. We find this name used in a song of praise credited to King David the warrior, songwriter, and poet. You may recognize the words: "The LORD is my light and my salvation – whom shall I fear?" (Psalm 27:1). The words *Lord* and *light* combine in this passage to form another descriptive name for God, Jehovah Ori, literally "the Lord [is] my light." This name is indeed unique. Keil and Delitzsch point out that this "infinitely profound name for God... is found only in this passage."[21] The phrase can be understood in a couple of ways. Obviously, associating God's name with light has to do with overcoming and dispelling the fear of darkness, but it can also be used to refer to divine guidance. Like a flashlight guiding us through the house when a storm knocks out our electricity, God is our light guiding us along the way.

David saw Jehovah Ori as a light guiding him through life. Another well-known psalm uses the same Hebrew word for *light* in the context of guiding. "Your word is a lamp for my feet, a light on my path" (Psalm 119:105). So although the specific description is used only in Psalm 27:1, the principle of God as our light runs throughout Scripture. Micah 7:8 says "The LORD will be my light."

Read the rest of Psalm 27. The reason David took courage in God as his guide was that it was difficult for David to find direction in the middle of the heavy circumstances that so often surrounded him. David's path was cluttered with wicked men advancing, "enemies" and "foes" attacking (Psalm 27:2), an army besieging, and war breaking out against him (v. 3). Which way should he go? Who could he trust? Would his fears be realized? All these questions were answered in the name of Jehovah Ori. David had learned that there was only one way to navigate without being afraid or becoming lost, and that was by having his Guide to light the way.

HOW WE GET LOST

At one time or another, you've probably experience what it's like to be lost. The good news for drivers these days is that it's probable you won't be lost for long. With our GPS technology, just one wrong turn and your car's device will declare (in a somewhat patronizing tone), "Recalculating." This is then followed by some instructions on how to head in the right direction. This very valuable tool assures us that even if we get lost, we will soon be back on track.

But how do we get lost in the first place? I think there are four common causes for getting lost.

Not listening

Sometimes we get lost because we didn't listen closely to the directions. Have you ever halfheartedly paid attention to a friend's directions about how to get to a wedding reception, only to find yourself driving down an unfamiliar street thirty minutes into a ten-minute trip?

"Did he say turn left at the second stop light or the second left right after the stop light… or was it a right after all?" Since my short attention span sometimes causes me to tune out in the middle of getting directions, I've found it's much easier just to follow a car whose driver knows where he is going. But when I do ask, I need to listen.

Receiving poor directions

Sometimes being lost is a result of getting poor directions. For the past seventeen years, I've lived in Normal, Illinois. In that time I have been stopped more than once while jogging during the late summer months. Inevitably some out-of-town parent who is bringing a freshman student to one of the town's universities slows the car down right next to me and asks, "Excuse me sir. Do you know how to get to Watterson Towers?"

Of course I know, but as a runner I really don't want to stop, nor am I thinking clearly. As a Christian, however, I usually feel the Spirit's nudge to stop and help. So while sweating profusely, breathing heavily, and sometimes jogging in place, I give them some quick directions and return to my exercise. I can't tell you the number of times I have realized as they've pulled away that I gave wrong directions. Because of my lack of focus, I simply did not communicate well what I knew.

These innocent people likely ended up lost on my account. Instead of asking me for directions, it would have been better for them to follow the big red mascot painted on the streets during university "move in" weekend. I should just reply, "Follow the cardinals!" It's important to ask directions from someone who really knows the way and will give good directions.

Not asking

Sometimes being lost is a matter of not asking for directions at all. How many family vacations have been complicated because the dad, insulted that his family would even suggest that they are lost, stubbornly refuses to pull over and ask for some guidance? My very unscientific hypothesis is that every male has a genetic inclination to refuse to ask for directions. It's not that we don't know we are lost; it's just that we are sure we'll find the way!

In the end, however, I must admit that stopping to ask for directions saves a lot of time and turmoil. In fact, when no one is around to suggest that I stop, I usually do stop and ask. (Don't tell anybody.)

The problem, of course, is pride. Humans in general don't like to admit their need for help, depend on someone else, or be told what to do. So we go on our respective merry (and lost) ways, pridefully insisting that we'll eventually figure things out.

Ignoring directions

Finally, sometimes people get lost because they ignore directions altogether. Recently, I was traveling with some friends through the mountains around Denver, Colorado. Our rental car was equipped with a GPS, into which we had entered the address of our destination. We knew the way to Denver, but about halfway through the two-hour trip, the female voice started chirping about exiting the highway we were on. Repeatedly, we ignored her commands; and each time we did, the estimated time for the trip increased.

"She must be wrong," we reasoned. We finally muted her. We had directions but ignored them.

GOD'S EPS"

When the Israelites left Egypt for the trip across the desert, through the Red Sea, and eventually through more desert toward

Mount Sinai, God didn't give directions; he gave his people a holy, personal escort. Probably because he knew that the Israelite people and their leaders would get lost in some of the same ways we have mentioned ("Did God say left at the Red Sea or right?"), Jehovah Ori literally guided them by lighting their way out of Egypt and toward the promised land. In what I like to call God's EPS (Eternal Positioning System), he illuminated a pillar of cloud and pillar of fire for them to follow. When leading two to three million people, you don't want to get lost, and God ensured that they wouldn't.

"By day the LORD went ahead of them in a pillar of cloud to guide them on their way and by night in a pillar of fire to give them light, so that they could travel by day or night. Neither the pillar of cloud by day nor the pillar of fire by night left its place in front of the people (Exodus 13:21, 22). All that the people of God had to do was follow the direction of the cloud and the fire. Getting lost was not possible – or so it seemed.

> **When leading two to three million people, you don't want to get lost, and God ensured that they wouldn't.**

Can you imagine the chaos of this freedom caravan? Two to three million people were leaving Egypt with everything they owned in tow. They took all their tents, clothes, and cooking utensils – and U-Haul did not exist. These recently freed slaves included newborn babies and aged family patriarchs. Everything from strollers to wheelchairs. No doubt the young, strong men showed off by carrying heavy loads on their shoulders. Kids were running around and playing tag. Babies were crying. Trumpets were blowing. Tribal banners were displayed. Everyone was filled with joy as this glorious day unfolded.

My guess is that this elation lasted for about one mile!

As they continued traveling into the desert on the initial day of their trip, the sun grew hot and the sand burned their feet. Some wondered, *Exactly where is Moses taking us?* Others were already shouting instructions, telling Moses and Aaron where they should turn and questioning their choice of direction. (Imagine what they might have thought when they eventually turned south toward the Red Sea, toward a dead end! See Exodus 13:18.) Still others must have complained about the pace of the journey and being too tired to continue. Surely at some point someone asked, "Are we there yet?" Wouldn't they have been shocked to know they would not be "there" for another forty years!

This group needed a way to move together in the same direction toward the promised land. But how? God developed a simple plan for guidance: follow the cloud by day and the fire by night. God was the perfect Guide as he led them to the destination he had prepared for them.

Believe it or not, even though God provided the pillar of cloud by day and fire by night for forty years, these people lost their way many times. Maybe you can relate.

HOW WE GET LOST – SPIRITUALLY

When it comes to getting spiritual directions, we get lost for many of the same reasons we've already mentioned. Even though our God is the Guide who provides the best possible direction for our lives, we, like the children of Israel, often lose our way. But how can this be so? Hint: It has to do with the way in which we respond to our Guide, Jehovah Ori.

Not listening

Sometimes God's people are lost because they haven't listened to their Guide closely enough. Some followers of Christ get lost because they follow only the parts of God's directions that suit them. Sometimes they simply have not spent enough time with his directions. Even those who are familiar with the teachings of the Bible can sometimes miss God's deeper truths because they are content to listen only at an elementary level. Many of the same Christians who sing praise songs on Sunday, put money in the offering plate, and have a Christian fish on their car's bumper do not pay close attention to the directions God gives in the bible. They may overindulge in food and drink, allow sexual images to be imprinted onto their minds through movies and the Internet, and gossip about someone they go to church with.

If you are thinking, *Well, "those people" aren't very good Christians,* I agree. But I hope you're talking about yourself as well as others. Jesus said, "Let anyone of you who is without sin be the first to throw a stone" (John 8:7). We all miss the way from time to time, don't we?

God has given us complete and perfect directions in his written Word. Only by following his commands will we truly find our way. Make no mistake – he does have definitive rules and guidelines for marriage, family, finances, work, play, relationships, celebrations, and conflicts. Rather than holding a bunch of rules over our heads, "his commands are not burdensome" (1 John 5:3). God is simply showing us the way. Yet many Christ followers struggle to find their way in stress-filled marriages, dysfunctional families, all-consuming work, unfulfilling play, and fleeting celebrations. They are lost because they have not paid attention to the light in the written Word of their Guide.

Receiving poor directions

Of course, poor directions can come from people who are not following God at all. But we must also be aware of the temptation to follow the advice given as God's guidance by a well-meaning brother or sister in Christ, when the direction given is counter to God's Word. For instance, I know of direction like this that was given during a weekly men's prayer group. When a man in the group shared the pain he was going through because of his wife's obvious and repeated infidelity, one brother suggested they pray for him to have the strength to love her unconditionally, as Christ loved us.

While this sounds very spiritual, it would, in fact, enable the wayward wife to continue in her sinful ways. The advice was so convicting and the prayer time they experienced was so powerful that the man continued to "love" his wife in spite of her sin – thinking he was following God's will.

In fact, he should have biblically confronted his wife and called her into account for her sins, per the direction given in Matthew 18:15-19 and 1 Corinthians 5:1-5.

When groups of Christians assemble and begin giving advice to others, an important and helpful clarifying statement to keep in mind is this: "Let's see if we can find some biblical teaching to support that idea." Following this guideline will help assure that the directions of Christian friends are coming from the Guide, Jehovah Ori.

Not asking

Others lack direction because they didn't ask God to guide them at all. James, the half-brother of Jesus and an early church leader in Jerusalem, wrote, "If any of you lacks wisdom, you should ask God, who gives generously to all without finding fault, and it will be given to you" (James 1:5). James also said, "You do not have because you do not ask God" (4:2). Jesus would agree, as he encouraged us to "ask and it will be given to you; seek and you will find; knock and the door will be opened to you" (Matthew 7:7). Direction is available if we ask.

Sometimes we decide to go on this journey alone. Day after day we attempt to accomplish things in our own strength. When trouble comes, we strategize ways to fix the situation. As the bills mount, we figure out how to make more money or consolidate our payments. When we are at wit's end with our teenagers, we pool our collective ignorance with others for ways to change them. When we do not have joy in our souls, we plan fun events to get an emotional boost.

Like the dad who insists on finding his own way even though he is undeniably lost, we persist in driving through life our own way, ignoring the signs that we are farther from our destination than we've ever been... but hoping somehow to arrive.

> **Sometimes we decide to go on this journey alone. Day after day we attempt to accomplish things in our own strength. When trouble comes, we strategize ways to fix the situation.**

What might happen if we (or our friends) suggested, "Let's pray for God to give guidance for this challenge"? After prayer, we might continue to look for God's direction in a Bible verse or testimony that connects with our situation, and thus allow God to shed his light in a very real and practical way.

Ignoring directions

Finally, there are many who desire Jesus as their Savior, but not as their Lord. These people may love coming to church, enjoy the worship, sense the presence of the Spirit, like the preaching, and feel accepted by those in the church. They may even desire to *join* the church – but they are not willing to allow God to guide them.

A recurring challenge we have in our ministry is the number of people who want to live together before they are married. I have met with many of these couples who say they want to follow Jesus, but they just don't see the harm of living together (especially since they say they are not involved in sexual activity).

I encourage them to consider the dangers of flirting with temptation, as Proverbs 6:27 asks, "Can a man scoop fire into his lap without his clothes being burned?" I also remind them that others (including their children, if they already have them) may get wrong impressions that will negatively influence their walk with the Lord. First Thessalonians 5:22 warns us: "Abstain from all appearance of evil" (*KJV*).

In spite of understanding the biblical directions, many of these couples ignore them and refuse to stop living together. It is no wonder that they get lost on their spiritual journey. They have refused to follow the Guide.

OUR TRUSTWORTHY GUIDE

Jehovah Ori is a trustworthy Guide because he never leaves us on our own, and he does not give wrong directions. This Guide David sang about in Psalm 27:1 illustrated his guiding quality by leading his people out of Egypt. He did not want them to get lost. Perhaps the best part of his guiding in our lives is that he has never misguided anyone. If we will simply follow him, we will arrive at the right destination and right on time.

Day and night

Reread Exodus 13:33. There is no instance of a nighttime march recorded for us in Scripture, but we are told in this verse that they *could* travel by night because the pillar of fire was there. In the future as they journeyed beyond the Red Sea, maybe God moved his people in the night from time to time so that they would avoid enemies. For forty years, while millions of Israelites slept in their tents, God's guiding presence was visible from anywhere in the camp.

Imagine a little Hebrew child waking up scared due to a bad dream or a clap of thunder. Mom and Dad could simply pull back the flap on the tent opening and say, "You see that fire over there? That's God's presence. Now go to sleep. God is right here with us."

Much of our journey feels like nighttime travel. The day is less intimidating. Those events in our lives that we might classify as "daytime travel" are obviously lighted by God's presence. We see his guiding blessing in joyous family weddings, job promotions, making the team, getting a bonus, and enjoying an evening meal with the family. It's easy to feel God's guidance during those times.

But let's be honest – a lot of this journey takes place during the nighttime. When we find ourselves stumbling along in the darkness of cancer, death, failure, conflict, broken relationships, and uncertainty about the future, God's guiding presence remains – even if it isn't as apparent as a pillar of fire. He is the constant night-light, a security for his people. The Lord of light has illustrated that he's with us, acting as Guide, whether it's day or night.

Unconditional love

Jehovah Ori is a trustworthy Guide because he loves us. God guided the Israelites to the promised land for one reason: he loved them. He made a promise to Abraham that he and his descendants would be God's chosen people. About a thousand years after the exodus, the book of Nehemiah recalls how love had prompted God to act on their behalf: "Because of your great compassion you did not abandon them in the wilderness. By day the pillar of cloud did not fail to guide them on their path, nor the pillar of fire by night to shine on the way they were to take" (Nehemiah 9:19).

That verse was part of a priestly prayer of repentance offered on behalf of God's people. Their disobedience had landed them captive in Babylon, and subsequently, God's mercy had returned them to their homeland. Ezra, Nehemiah, and the Levites had read God's Word to the people and encouraged them (Nehemiah 8). The prayer then proclaimed God's ongoing faithfulness in loving his people – and the guidance he had given them all the way back to those desert wanderings confirming it. And God was being asked to forgive the people for not recognizing his love, for repeatedly ignoring his guidance, and for not loving him in return.

Guidance doesn't always feel like love. Most parents are motivated by love when they guide their children with rules and instructions.

But the curfews, the "No, you may nots," and the chores are often seen as restrictive, unreasonable, and even unloving. Most church leaders are motivated by a love for God's people when they make visionary decisions, but often there are those in the congregation who see it differently. Husbands are called to love their wives and lead them biblically, but even Christian wives can sometimes question motives behind a husband's decision making.

Because of our sinful nature, most humans don't like to simply submit and follow. Eve didn't, so she ate the forbidden fruit. We don't' so we touch walls that say, "Wet paint." There are no perfect human guides for our lives. Some are not motivated by love and, therefore, make oppressive rules. But our God is the perfect Guide. Because he loves us, we can trust his direction.

Perfect knowledge

Jehovah Ori is a trustworthy Guide because only he can light the way. The Old Testament people of God generally knew where they were heading. They could describe the land as "promised," "flowing with milk and honey," and "a land sworn to their forefathers." But they couldn't give the longitude and latitude coordinates. There was no address to enter into the Garmin on their camels. On the other hand, God knew precisely where they were going. He knew the exact boundaries and every square mile by heart. God was aware of potential enemies and difficult terrain. This knowledge made him the perfect guide, so he escorted them to their destination. He literally lighted their way.

Again, the book of Nehemiah referred back to those times when the priests' prayer confessed with all Israel: "By day you led them with a pillar of cloud, and by night with a pillar of fire to give them light on the way they were to take" (Nehemiah 9:12). The word "light" in this verse is *ori*.

God's motivation for leading us is to light a spiritual path for our everyday living. In a general sense, we know where we are going. Like our spiritual forefathers, we can describe our ultimate destination; we use phrases like "streets of gold," "in God's presence," "eternal life," and "multitudes gathered around the throne." But we really don't know what turns, detours, and rest stops we might take along the way. God, however, knows our journey completely. He knows the number of days we have and the things those days will be filled with. He doesn't show us the whole map at once – all the details of the journey – because it would be too intimidating for us. He simply desires to shine light on our way as we follow him each day on the journey.

HIS GUIDING PRESENCE

If God led his people with a pillar of fire and a pillar of cloud back in the day, how does he guide your life today?

Though I haven't seen a pillar above the houses of any Christ followers I know, he has not left us without directions to light our paths on the journey.

Through his Son

In prophesying about the coming Messiah, Isaiah provided the image of people lost on the journey, when he said, "The people walking in darkness have seen a great light; on those living in the land of deep darkness a light has dawned" (Isaiah 9:2). The apostle John added to this imagery when he said, "In him was life, and that life was the light of all mankind... The true light that gives light to everyone was coming into the world" (John 1:4, 9). Jehovah Ori did not send a pillar to guide us; he gave his Son instead.

Jesus' simple call to his followers was, "Follow me." After all, like our guide at the White House he's been here before. Jesus said in John 14:6, "I am the way" (literally, the road). Ultimately, following

Jesus is the right direction for all of us, for our entire lives. No matter what your journey has been or where you are heading, he is the light who can guide you in the way you should go.

- Do you need to start over? Let Jesus be your guide.
- Do you need to forgive? Let Jesus be your guide.
- Do you need hope for tomorrow? Let Jesus be your guide.
- Do you want to live, really live? Let Jesus be your guide.
- Do you want to spend eternity with the Father? Let Jesus be your guide.

Through his Word

He guides us by the light of his written Word. Jesus is the *living* Word of God (John 1:1-3), but we also have the *written* Word of God, the Bible, as a daily guide for our lives. King Solomon wrote of the Scriptures he was teaching, "This command is a lamp, this teaching is a light" (Proverbs 6:23). The words from the longest psalm in the Bible remind us how the Word of God guides us: "I gain understanding from your precepts; therefor I hate every wrong path. Your word is a lamp for my feet, a light on my path" (Psalm 119:104, 105).

This travel language reminds us that there is no guide for life's journey like the written Word of God. It is applicable to all people in all places at all times.

- Do you need guidance in your parenting? Read the Bible.
- Do you need peace from the stress of life? Read the Bible.
- Do you need assurance that it's going to be all right? Read the Bible.
- Do you need direction for how to use all that God has entrusted to you? Read the Bible.

Through his Holy Spirit

Finally, Jehovah Ori guides those who have chosen to follow
him through the presence of his Holy Spirit living in them. Jesus
is God's guidance fleshed out, the Bible is God's guidance spoken,
and the Spirit is God's guidance living in us! Just like the pillar of
cloud and pillar of fire, the Spirit never goes away. Night and day he
is there – moving within us to change us, to convict us, to comfort
us, and to guide us. Jesus spoke of his coming: "When he, the Spirit
of truth, comes, he will guide you into all the truth" (John 16:13).
The apostle Paul spoke of "the Spirit of wisdom" and prayed that the
eyes of believers' hearts "may be enlightened in order that you may
know the hope to which he has called you" (Ephesians 1:17, 18). This
word "enlightened" is the Greek *phōtizō* and is the same root used
to translate Jehovah Ori in the Greek translation of Psalm 27:1.[22]
Remarkably, this Scripture ties Jehovah Ori (God the Guide who
sheds light for our paths) to the Holy Spirit (God's presence shining
light in our hearts).

As believers, we have 24/7 guidance available through the Spirit's
presence in our lives.

Do you need help praying? Ask the Spirit to guide you.

Are you facing a tough conversation? Ask the Spirit to intervene.

Are you in conflict with a brother or sister in Christ? Ask the
Spirit to guide you in peace.

Are you struggling to make a major decision? Seek the Spirit's
leading.

AN AMAZING GUIDE

On a short-term mission trip to Nairobi, Kenya, a young man
learned how God often leads. Mike had spent his week helping with
a medical clinic and serving the poor in whatever way he could. Near
the end of the trip, there was a time of gift giving to some of the

neediest of the families – in the squatters' slum. As this gathering was drawing to a close, the festivities were interrupted by gunfire and tear gas that quickly dispersed the people. The missionary who was present hurriedly scooted the Americans into a van and insisted that they leave immediately. His only instruction was to pray.

As Mike and the others prayed in the van, they went from being shaken and eager to leave, to being filled with peace. In the midst of the chaos surrounding them, they felt like they were supposed to be there and that God would protect them. Mike was led to Psalm 27, which he read several times. A Kenyan national informed him that this was the text for a sermon preached during a former persecution against those living in the slum.

Upon his return to the U.S., Mike discovered that while his team had been in the midst of the turmoil in Kenya, a pastor from his church had led a time of prayer for them, during which they prayed and read… Psalm 27. By his Spirit God had guided those on both sides of the ocean to Psalm 27. For Mike's team, the Lord was their light and salvation during a potentially dark time.

A good guide makes all the difference. It's true of trips, tours, and destinations – and it's even truer of the spiritual life. Jehovah Ori is the Lord of light. He provided guidance for the Israelites on their long journey to the promised land. He provides direction today for Christians on a journey to their promised reward. He will guide us through each and every turn along the way. The only way to get lost is to ignore the faithful direction of Jehovah Ori.

FIRST-NAME BASIS
For individual or group study

1. What do you rely on most for traveling directions?
   _____ a physical map
   _____ directions from a friend
   _____ seek and hope to find
   _____ GPS
   _____ being "talked through" the last few miles via cell phone?

   Why do you prefer this method?

2. Have you ever been lost? What happened? How did you find your way back to the right path? What emotions did you feel when you didn't know where you were? When you've gotten lost, were you more likely to stop immediately and ask for directions or just keep going and try to figure it out? Why?

3. Have you ever (figuratively and spiritually speaking) made a wrong turn in your life? What happened? Why do you think you made this turn? What was the result?

4. When have you needed some direction in life and you sought God's guidance? What other methods did you seek out, trying to find direction? What was the result?

GETTING ACQUAINTED WITH
JEHOVAH ORI

1. Spend some time reflecting (focused thinking with an awareness of God's presence) on these directional phrases:

   A wrong turn I regret most...
   The part of my life that feels "lost" to me right now is...
   I need guidance for the future when it comes to...

Don't rush to complete those statements. Read them aloud. Invite God to read them with you, and pray through them as you read.

2. Write each of those three incomplete statements on an index card and put the cards in a place where you will see them many times throughout the day. Again, don't rush to fill them in; just continue to chew on them.

3. When you have spent several hours/days considering the statements, complete them by writing down one or two things for each. Now consider this narrowed list. Don't rush to resolve them; simply own where you are.

4. After several more days, consult a Bible concordance for verses that speak to the things you have written down.

5. Keep you index cards handy. As you read the Bible, note any verse that gives you direction for each situation.

6. Seek God's forgiveness for times in which you have taken your own path.

7. Confess Psalm 27:1 aloud several times; then pray for the guiding light of God's Holy Spirit to direct your paths.

God who saves
El Moshaah El Mow.shah.ah

Some versions render El Moshaah as God of *deliverances* or God of *salvation*. We must "put our hope in the living God, who is the Savior of all people" (1 Timothy 4:10).

SEVEN

SAVIOR
{1 Samuel 11:1-15; Psalm 68:20}

JERRY BRIDGES

One of the best-kept secrets among Christians today is this: Jesus paid it all. I mean all. He not only purchased your forgiveness of sins and your ticket to Heaven, He purchased every blessing and every answer to prayer you will ever receive.

The situation felt really hopeless. I was disappointed because I was ready to go home but the plane we were supposed to take had still not arrived. It had been raining sideways all day, with winds gusting up to fifty miles an hour. The small planes that typically flew into this low-tech regional airport wouldn't stand a chance against the elements on this morning. Still I prayed for God to miraculously stop the rain, find a plane, and direct it to me (OK, it was a very selfish prayer). I was convinced that if my wife and I could just make our connecting flight to the big city airport we were supposed to fly through, I had a chance of sleeping in my own comfortable bed that night.

But I wasn't really surprised when our host said the flight had been cancelled due to inclement weather. After a short pity party during our mud-soaked journey back to my friend's house, I decided to make the best of it by working on my sermon for Sunday.

After lunch I raided my host's small but adequate library of Bible commentaries and made my way to an upstairs room, with Bible and notepad in hand. My wife contacted our sons to inform them that we wouldn't be home as scheduled, then spent time with the lady of the house while I retreated into sermon preparation world.

The sound of the rain was actually peaceful as I read and jotted down a page full of thoughts and preaching possibilities. I actually remember thinking that God had turned it into a pretty good day after all, and I comforted myself with the fact that I would be home in less than twenty-four hours.

Then the walls of the house began to shake, and books I had been studying vibrated off the table and onto the floor. I'm a Midwest guy, but I knew we had just experienced an earthquake. I texted my son: "You won't believe it. First monsoon rains and now we just experienced an earthquake… what next?"

Admittedly, this story is of only mild interest at this point (or maybe of no interest at all). But what if told you that the day all this happened was January 12, 2010 and that my friend (a pastor) was hosting us in Cap-Haitian, a northern town in Haiti?

Yes, my wife and I (and part of a team from our church) had actually experienced the international event now referred to simply as the Haiti earthquake. But initially we had no clue that this incident was as catastrophic as it turned out to be. In fact, it was only because I broke my own mission-trip rule of not watching television (hey, the mission trip was technically over) that I discovered that CNN was covering the event. Four hours after the quake, we saw the footage of the devastation and realized that this was a rescue situation of worldwide interest.

There would be *no* flight out of Haiti the next day (or for many days to come). We had no way of communicating with the outside world, no idea how we were going to get home, and still no real indication of just how serious this all was. But as we gathered around to see the first pictures of the damage, we knew that our rescue was much less important than the circumstances of those desperate people who were in the capital of Port-au-Prince (the airport I had prayed for God to get us to!).

Soon we turned off the TV and talked to the only one who could save us and the only one who could save the people of Haiti. We prayed to El Moshaah, our God who saves.

THE GOD WHO SAVES

In the Jewish psalms, we find a praise song written by King David that names God as one who can rescue. "Our God is a God who saves; from the Sovereign Lord comes escape from death" (Psalm 68:20). The phrase "God who saves" consists of two Hebrew words: *el* and *moshaah*. *El* is the shortened version of the name Elohim that we studied in Chapter 1 of this book. Here it is paired with the word *moshaah,* which literally means "saving act," "deliverance," or "salvation."[23] Though this is the only place these words combine to give us this title for God in the Hebrew Scriptures, the idea of salvation is associated with God throughout the Old Testament, including in Psalm 69:19, the verse just preceding the one quoted above. "In his rule he vindicates and protects. The activity of vindication and protection finds expression in the repeated use of the root [*yasha*] ("save"): 'God our Saviour' (v. 19; lit., 'the God who saves') (v. 20; lit., 'God of salvations')[24]

The word *yasha* is a significant word (translated as *save, deliver,* or *rescue*) that describes God's saving ability regarding his covenant people. The word is used 209 times in the Old Testament.[25] Here is just a sampling:

- "That day the LORD *saved* Israel from the hands of the Egyptians, and Israel saw the Egyptians lying dead on the shore" (Exodus 14:30).
- "When you go into battle in your own land against an enemy who is oppressing you, sound a blast on the trumpets. Then you will be remembered by the Lord your God and *rescued* from your enemies" (Numbers 10:9).
- "Blessed are you, Israel! Who is like you, a people *saved* by the LORD? He is your shield and helper and your glorious sword" (Deuteronomy 33:29).
- "Then the LORD raised up judges, who *saved* them out of the hands of these raiders" (Judges 2:16).
- "As surely as the LORD who *rescues* Israel lives…" (1 Samuel 14:39).
- "Turn, LORD, and deliver me; *save* me because of your unfailing love" (Psalm 6:4).
- "When you, God, rose up to judge, to *save* all the afflicted of the land…" (76:9).
- "He *saved* them for his name's sake, to make his mighty power known" (106:8).
- "Surely the arm of the LORD is not too short to *save*, nor his ear too dull to hear" (Isaiah 59:1).
- "Heal me, LORD, and I will be healed; *save* me and I will be *saved*, for you are the one I praise" (Jeremiah 17:14, emphasis added in all).

SURROUNDED

In the earliest stages of his kingship, Saul acted as the Lord's anointed to save a city in Israel. The story begins with the people of

God in dire circumstances. Nahash the Ammonite had attacked the Israelite town of Jabesh Gilead (1 Samuel 11:1), which was a town on the east side of the Jordan River. "The Ammonites were descended from Lot... and lived east of the Jordan River and south of the Jabbok."²⁶ On more than one occasion in the Israelites' history, a neighbor-enemy like Nahash was emboldened to attack the loosely organized people of Israel who had been led for a hundred years only by the occasional judge. The judges were God's way of saving his people during these years when Israel had no king (see Judges 2:16).

Saul's coronation celebration had been a joyous occasion, but it seems as if life for the first anointed king of Israel and the people of God had returned to normal. After Saul made an agreement with the people, Samuel sent them home; and Saul also returned to his hometown in Gibeah (1 Samuel 10:25, 26).

Perhaps Nahash had not heard that the Hebrew nation now had a king (Saul couldn't update his status to "king" since there was no Facebook in those days), or maybe Nahash just wasn't afraid of this new leader. Whatever the case, Nahash advanced against the city of Jabesh Gilead with his army and, in no time, had the city surrounded. Realizing that they didn't have an organized army and that their newly anointed king had returned to work in the fields of his hometown of Gibeah, the elders made the only wise decision they could. In essence, they surrendered, offering to become subject to Nahash and his people (11:1). This would mean submitting to Nahash's authority and paying some sort of tax to him. It would be completely humiliating to the proud Israelite men, but they had no choice if they wanted to live.

Usually this kind of offer was agreeable to an aggressive king since it would feed his ego and increase his wealth without losing a single warrior from his army. Nahash, however, sought to raise the stakes with the men of Jabesh Gilead, offering this alarming response: "I will make a treaty with you only on the condition that I gouge out the right eye of every one of you and so bring disgrace on all Israel" (v. 2).

Some scholars see this counteroffer as an allusion to the practice of cutting or mutilation involved in the ancient Near East when two parties made a covenant. The men of Jabesh Gilead "asked Nahash to 'make a treaty' (v. 1, lit., 'cut a covenant') with them… The phrase 'cut a covenant' is almost universally understood to refer to the sacrifice ('cutting') of one or more animals as an important element in covenant solemnization ceremonies."[27] In other words, Nahash may have indicated that the men of Jabesh would serve as the mutilated sacrificial confirmation themselves! He may also have been punishing them for breaking a previous covenant."[28]

While both are possibilities, we can't ignore the actual words of Nahash's threat that reveal his desire to disgrace Israel. As painful as the gouging out of an eye would be, the pain of dishonor brought by this foreign king's mutilating the men of an entire Israelite town would have been emotionally debilitating. Additionally, these men would have been physically weaker to defend their homes against future attacks. Imagine the disadvantage in hand-to-hand combat for the soldier with one eye.

Whatever Nahash's full reasons for making this offer, it put the people of Jabesh Gilead in a position of desperation. This stipulation tacked onto their surrender was more than they had bargained for; but again, they didn't seem to have much choice against this powerful enemy.

So they did the best thing they could think of – they bought some time and looked for a savior. The elders of Jabesh told Nahash, "Give us seven days so we can send messengers throughout Israel; if no one comes to rescue us, we will surrender to you" (v. 3). Arrogantly, Nahash gave them permission to look for someone to save them. Quickly, they chose messengers and sent them to all the tribes of Israel in their various locations.

DESPERATE

This was a desperate mission with a simple plea: "Is there anyone who will come to save us now?" This is a great question for us today. Is there anyone who will come to save us? Is there anyone who can rescue us from the respective situations in which we find ourselves? It's certainly a question we asked in the midst of the Haiti earthquake. Who might come to rescue those who were homeless, hungry, or injured?

More importantly, this question has spiritual significance. As we journey with Jesus, we often find ourselves in the same predicament as these men of Jabesh Gilead. We identify sin as our enemy easily enough, but we sometimes feel overpowered by it and surrender to its influence, knowing all the while that it will end in spiritual enslavement and pain.

> **So they did the best thing they could think of – they bought some time and looked for a savior.**

We are not alone. Apparently, even apostles faced this feeling of helplessness in their daily walk with God. Paul spoke of this in the New Testament in a completely transparent discussion of his personal struggle with sin. In Romans 7 he described the battle between the mind and the flesh and how the flesh often seems to prevail. "For I do not do the good I want to do," he observed, "but the evil I do not want to do – this I keep on doing" (Romans 7:19). This led him to proclaim, "What a wretched man I am! Who will rescue me from this body that is subject to death?"

In the very next verse he provided the answer: Jesus Christ our Lord.

There is a continuous awareness for Christ followers that the battle against sin is real and that we often feel as if we are losing. There are some people who believe this struggle with sin that Paul is talking of is a description of his life *before* Jesus instead of his ongoing battle with sin as a believer, but I believe it is both. Throughout my twenty-seven years as a pastor, I've been in on many conversations concerning people's real-life struggles. The following two cases are compilations of the lives I've encountered and hundreds of conversations I've had. The actual names have been changed.

Nick, a senior in high school, is a great Christian teenager. He feels a calling to preach and is contemplating attending Bible college. He regularly leads home group Bible studies, started his school's prayer group, and has baptized four of his friends in the last three months. He truly loves the Lord, but he doesn't feel like it as he sits in my office and tears of regret fill his eyes. He can't seem to shake the lure of pornography that has become a part of his world. He has prayed Psalm 51 a million times. He has claimed 1 John 1:9 and the forgiveness that it promises. He knows that the Spirit of God lives in him as guide. But still, when he finds himself alone at home, all too often he is downloading sexual images of lust.

He wants to stop this sin. He has tried to battle this by several means: accountability partners, fasting from media, and Scripture memorization. But this one sin seems to continually find its way back into his life. He feels helpless against this temptation as he asks, "Will this struggle ever go away?" he wants to know if he can be saved from lust.

Mandy left a quick message on my phone. She needed to talk to her pastor as soon as possible. Usually in this situation, I would refer a member of the opposite sex to another Christian woman, but since she wanted to talk to me specifically, I agreed to meet with her with my wife present. Mandy is a middle-aged dynamo, teaches the Sunday school class for two-year-olds, greets everyone with a smile, and is the first to volunteer when help is needed. She is pretty from the inside out, but she has a secret.

She begins, "I have been bulimic for twenty years, and I don't think this is honoring to God." She goes on to say that ever since her "chubby phase" in high school (when some classmates poked fun at her); she has secretly induced vomiting to keep her weight down. She knows that God and her husband both see her as beautiful, and she truly wants to stop. She has seen a Christian counselor, read numerous books, and "repented a million times." But again and again she returns to this destructive behavior (including on the morning that we met). Through tears she wonders, "Will I ever conquer this sinful behavior?" She wants to know if someone can save her from her sin of focusing on outward beauty.

IN MOURNING

Just as the Ammonite king Nahash threatened to enslave and disable the men of Jabesh Gilead, sin is the enemy in our lives that threatens to bring us harm and take away our freedom. Sin is a constant evil from which we need to be saved.

When the messengers from Jabesh Gilead crossed the Jordan to the west and headed south, they came to the town of Gibeah. In our day a sign outside the city would have read, "Welcome to Gibeah, hometown of Saul, the king of Israel." But these people didn't have any more confidence than the rest of the tribes, even though the new king lived there. The messengers relayed their predicament to the elders of the city anyway. "When the messengers… reported these terms to the people, they all wept aloud" (1 Samuel 11:4).

When Saul came home for the evening, no one had to tell him that the people were upset; he could see for himself that the whole town was in tears. They were likely upset because they assumed that if Nahash could threaten the town of Jabesh Gilead, it would only be a matter of time before he would threaten Gibeah too. So they mourned.

> **Through tears she wonders, "Will I ever conquer this sinful behavior?"**

Similarly, we face daily threats from our enemy Satan as he attempts to shake our confidence and our faith. First Peter 5:8 tells us that he is literally seeking to devour us, and like Nahash, his favorite way to devour us spiritually is through fear. He seeks to make us afraid of our mortality and death. He brings worries to mind about our future. He stirs up fears of loneliness and not belonging. But one of the biggest threats he brings our way is through temptation. We may fear a particular sin and the hold it seems to have over us. There are times in which we feel that there is no hope of winning the battle, no rescue from the power of sin and temptation.

SOUND THE ALARM

Just as El Moshaah had a plan to save his people in Jabesh Gilead, he has always had a plan to save us. According to Numbers 10:9, when we begin to feel overwhelmed in the battle against sin, the first thing we should do is "sound a blast on the trumpets. Then you will be remembered by the Lord your God and rescued from your enemies."

In the account of 1 Samuel 11, Saul went about it in a different way. We are not told that he blew a trumpet; instead he cut up a pair of oxen and sent the pieces via messengers throughout Israel's territories – and with a very strong message: "This is what will be done to the oxen of anyone who does not follow Saul and Samuel" (v. 7). When we are in need of a rescue, our first step should be to declare the seriousness of the situation and sound the alarm any way we can.

But rather than sounding the trumpet of war against our sin, how many times have we hidden our sins from others because we are so sure the battle is ours alone? I often reassure Christian men who feel like they are the only ones who struggle with lust that they are not alone. That is why a popular book is entitled *Every Man's Battle*. No one is immune. Everyone is in the battle against sin; no one is unique in this regard. The apostle Paul stated, "No temptation has overtaken you except what is common to mankind" (1 Corinthians 10:13).

Just as the people of God living in Jabesh Gilead were not left to fight on their own, we are not called to battle against sin on our own either. El Moshaah has a plan for saving us; but we must declare the battle, blow some trumpets, cut up some oxen… anything to name the battle and classify it as serious. Here are some practical ways in which we can blow the trumpets in regard to our battles.

- Talk to God about your sins. He knows them anyway. First John 1:9 promises, "If we confess our sins, he is faithful and just and will forgive us our sins and purify us from all unrighteousness."
- Acknowledge the enemies hindering your spiritual growth and tell God about them. Jesus taught us to pray about our temptations: "And lead us not into temptation, but deliver us from the evil one" (Matthew 6:13).
- Write the sins on paper. Physically writing out our spiritual struggles makes them easier to deal with head on. "If we claim we have not sinned, we make him out to be a liar, and his word is not in us" (I John 1:10).
- Tell a trusted Christian friend the sins you have acknowledged in your battle. This helps with accountability, and it sets the stage to wage war through prayer. "Therefore confess your sins to each other and pray for each other so that you may be healed. The prayer of a righteous person is powerful and effective" (James 5:16).
- When you sin, quickly call it what it is and repent. I have found that the quicker I verbally label it as sin between God and me (or others), the more clearly I see it for what it is: an enemy that can destroy me. This is why David prayed, "Against you, you only, have I sinned and done what is evil in your sight; so you are right in your verdict and justified when you judge" (Psalm 51:4).

THE WAY TO VICTORY

In his battle with Nahash, it is interesting to note that Saul had already sought God's help – as the presence of the Lord's prophet Samuel indicates. He was there at the end of the battle (see 1 Samuel 11:12), so it is likely he was present at the beginning. At this point in Saul's leadership, he understood that the battle belonged to the Lord. Later a shepherd boy named David would state the truth: "All those gathered here will know that it is not by sword or spear that the Lord saves; for the battle is the LORD'S, and he will give all of you into our hands" (1 Samuel 17:47).

No matter how many men showed up for this battle or how fiercely they fought, Saul was not the savior – El Moshaah was. As it turned out, "the men of Israel numbered three hundred thousand and those of Judah thirty thousand" (11:8). However, it was the saving power of God that brought about complete victory that day.

As Deuteronomy 33:29 indicates, the battle of salvation always belongs to God. We cannot save ourselves. The people of God have never saved themselves. It is the work of El Moshaah that overcomes our sin. The apostle Paul exclaimed the answer to his sin predicament: "Thanks be to God, who delivers me through Jesus Christ our Lord!" (Romans 7:25).

King Saul was the man whom God used to muster an army and rescue his people from Nahash, and Jesus is the man God used to rescue us from sin. All sin has been overcome through the blood of Jesus, once and for all. "Unlike the other high priests, he does not need to offer sacrifices day after day, first for his own sins, and then for the sins of the people. He sacrificed for their sins once and for all when he offered himself" (Hebrews 7:27). But still the battle against our enemy Satan rages on.

We daily go to battle in the strength of our God who saves. Not only has God provided ultimate rescue from sin through his Son; he is also there in the daily battle. He saves us from sin every time we face it and call out to him. The good news is this: "God is faithful; he will not let you be tempted beyond what you can bear. But when you are tempted, he will also provide a way out so that you can endure it" (1 Corinthians 10:13).

RESCUED DAY BY DAY

I had a friend in college who was socially awkward and had some strange practices. He often stopped conversation abruptly by suddenly closing his eyes and bowing his head. Whether he was in a dorm room with a bunch of guys, hiking on a mountain trail with friends, or sitting at a table in the cafeteria, he simply ended the conversation by checking out. I first thought he was crazy, but I discovered later that he was literally living out 1 Corinthians 10:13. Any time he identified a temptation to sin or a spiritual battle in his thoughts or words, he would stop immediately and ask God for a way out.

That kind of radical approach seemed weird and uncomfortable at times, but I respected him for his serious pursuit of holiness and his faith in the God who saves. What would happen if we prayed more spontaneous prayers when we sensed a need for rescue from a sin that we felt creeping in?

What would happen if we prayed more spontaneous prayers when we sensed a need for rescue from a sin that we felt creeping in?

After the army of 330,000 was assembled in Bezek, Saul sent word to the men of Jabesh Gilead, saying, "By the time the sun is hot tomorrow, you will be rescued" (1 Samuel 11:9). Of course, this was great news. They were going to be saved! They coyly told the men of Ammon that they would surrender at noon the next day.

That day never came for the army of Nahash. In the last watch of the night, Saul's army surprised the enemy before dawn and completely defeated them! The people of God had been saved, and God had used Saul to do it. Just before going on to Gilgal, where the people would officially affirm Saul as their king, Saul proclaimed, "This day the LORD has rescued Israel" (v. 13). He knew the supernatural source of their salvation.

Sometimes we miss the emotion of a Bible story because we know the ending, but for a moment try to imagine the quiet suspense of the people in Jabesh Gilead as they gathered in their homes the night before the battle. They were no less under siege by this formidable enemy, Nahash's army, but they had assurance of salvation. Because of this, there was no crying, mourning, or worrying about the consequences of surrender they had wept about only seven days earlier. Instead, there was an attitude of joy and thankfulness in the city as they anticipated victory and salvation. They knew that their enemy would be defeated.

We can view that night before the Israelites' victory as a metaphor for our spiritual lives. Like those people, we know the Savior. We are simply waiting for our salvation to be fully realized.

The victory over sin is sure. Jesus declared on the cross, "It is finished" (John 19:30). The enemy of death has been defeated. "Where, O death, is your victory? Where, O death is your sting?' The sting of death is sin, and the power of sin is the law. But thanks be to God! He gives us the victory through our Lord Jesus Christ" (1 Corinthians 15:55-57). We can proclaim along with the psalmist, "Our God is a God who saves; from the Sovereign LORD comes escape from death" (Psalm 68:20). His salvation and rescue stories are innumerable. Here's a small sampling of some recent ones I know about.

- The elder team at our church prayed early one Thursday morning for God to open doors for salvation in the lives of coworkers. Mid-afternoon that day, a coworker began a conversation about her need for Jesus. By the end of the day, she had accepted Christ by faith and was baptized the following Sunday.
- One of our church members who was rescued from a world of drugs and a nearly fatal suicide attempt faced extradition for crimes committed many years earlier in another state. One Sunday before he left, we prayed with him that God would rescue him from his past. A long bus ride terminated

at the police station, where he turned himself in. He spent one night in jail, but by the next day his public defender had gotten permission to transfer his probation back to our town. He was home and worshipping with us the next week.

- A group of ladies in our church were inspired to take Mother's Day gifts to some single moms – who happened to be dancers at a local strip club. The ladies had no connections to anyone at the club, just felt a nudging from the Holy Spirit to go. Days before they went, a local beauty shop called because they wanted to donate lotions and soaps for Mother's Day. These items filled the gift baskets for the women who were not expecting to be loved like this – especially from a church. A year later, the manager of that strip club and his girlfriend are now out of the adult entertainment industry and are baptized believers.

He is El Moshaah, the God who has rescued us and has saved us from our most dangerous enemy: sin. We can live confidently, even in our continual struggle against it, that sin is not an enemy to be feared. Until that day when faith becomes sight, we can sound the trumpets, seek the Lord, and wait confidently for the Savior to come and take us home.

In January 2010, we eventually arrived home from Haiti by taking a bus into the Dominican Republic and then flying home the next day. Rescue and relief efforts poured into Haiti – many of them because of caring Christians – and they still continue over two years after the event. I'm not sure that the physical needs of this impoverished and devastated island will ever be fully met, but on one Sunday a few weeks after the catastrophic earthquake, dozens were baptized into Christ at my friend's church in Haiti. They have been saved even as they continue to be rescued.

In that sense, we are like these Haitian brothers and sisters. El Moshaah has saved us, and we continue to be rescued by him every day.

FIRST-NAME BASIS
For individual or group study

1. Where were you when you heard of the Haiti earthquake (or some other major disaster)? What is your most enduring memory of that event?
2. Have you ever been in a situation (physically, financially, emotionally, or spiritually) where you felt like there was no way out? What was it like? How did that situation turn out?
3. If you have accepted Jesus as your Lord and Savior, what were the circumstances that caused you to come to a faith relationship with him?
4. Finish the following sentence with something specific, rather than just the word *sin*: "Jesus saved me from…" Personalize this statement according to your own experience. (For example, "Jesus has saved me from the materialistic pursuit that my corporate career had afforded me.") In what specific ways has this "saving" made a difference in your life?

GETTING ACQUAINTED WITH
EL MOSHAAH

1. Make a list of all the physical ailments, injuries, sicknesses, and diseases you can think of that you have personally experienced. Next to each, record how you were rescued from each. You may still be suffering from one or more of these. If that's the case, record what steps towards healing you have taken.
2. Contact a local nursing home or assisted-living facility and ask if there is a specific way your small group can help with the residents. Spend an afternoon or early evening in a rescue – ministering the comfort of El Moshaah through your presence companionship, conversation, and service with these precious people.

3. Trace or draw a picture of a trumpet on a sheet of construction paper or card stock. Cut out the trumpet. Then write on it the sins and spiritual struggles you face and desire to declare war against. Place this trumpet list where you can see it every morning and pray this prayer: "Lord, I declare war against these things today. Please save me by the power of your Son's blood as I follow you."

Meditate on 1 Corinthians 10:13; 1 John 1:9; and 1 Samuel 17:47. Record any battle victories on the back of the trumpet.

Ha Melek Jehovah Hah Meh.lek Jeh.ho.vuh

**The Hebrew word order is actually "the King the Lord,"
but less literal Bible translations use "the Lord the King."
The apostle Paul praised God as the "only Ruler, the
King of kings and Lord of lords" (I Timothy 6:15).**

EIGHT

King
{Psalm 98:6; I Samuel 8:1-22}

GENE EDWARDS

*I did not lift a finger to be made king. Nor shall I do so to preserve a kingdom.
Even the kingdom of God! God put me here. It is not my responsibility to take,
or keep, authority.*

This probably doesn't come as much of a surprise to you, if you
are a twenty-first century American, but I have never been in the
presence of a king. I have never been escorted into a grand hall with
a throne at one end. I have never knelt before royalty. I have never
uttered the words *Your Highness* (unless you count my being a smart
aleck with my wife or our boys when they've seemed demanding). I

have never had the opportunity to meet someone who has complete power and sovereignty over a country or a territory. I have never been around someone who is wearing a crown of real value that signifies authority. There are not – nor have there ever been – royal robes, scepters, decrees, or coronations in my world.

You might say that I'm a complete stranger to the concept of kingship. This may put me at a disadvantage as a Christian. After all, the Bible is filled with kingly talk, kingly rule, and kingly imagery. It might help if I could relate.

Don't get me wrong; I've *seen* plenty of kingly stuff. I have actually walked through the fifteenth-century compound called Topkapi Palace. "Between 1450 and 1465, shortly after his conquest of Constantinople, Mehmet II built Topkapi Palace as his principal residence."[29] This 550-year-old palace is actually an impressive complex of buildings, a great tourist destination in Istanbul, Turkey. The premises include Mehmet II's remarkably advanced kitchen and the centuries-old china used to serve his food. One can also see an incredible display of his armor, including diamond-studded swords, gem-covered armor made of gold, and an assortment of decorated helmets and crowns.

Mehmet II's palace grounds were surrounded by a wall (that still remains) and were situated on a cliff overlooking the sea. The complex included buildings for the king's harem, his library, a mosque, and his living quarters. Touring these historic grounds gives one a glimpse into the greatness of this once-powerful king.

I have also witnessed firsthand the remains of the palace compound of King Herod the Great in Caesarea. In my opinion, this is one of the most impressive archaeological sites in all Israel. Admittedly, the buildings have long been toppled and much of the complex has eroded into the sea over the past two thousand years, but the footprint of these structures gives indication of its first-century BC grandeur. Among other things the palace boasted a balcony with a view of the hippodrome so that Herod could watch the chariot races and games from a secure location (think of it as a luxury box). One can also see the foundational traces of a grand spa with hot baths and terraces that blended into the Mediterranean Sea (think infinity pool with a view to sunsets over the water).

The complex itself contained a great hall for judgments, trials, and other royal occasions, as well as the king's private living space and quarters for his soldiers. It was one of several palaces and fortresses built by Herod during his lifetime, including his residences in Jerusalem and Masada. Herod was called "the Great" partly because of his extensive building of cities and fortresses.

EARTHLY KINGS VS. *THE* KING

If you've never lived in a kingdom or been subject to a king, you may find it hard to fully relate to this final name for God that we will examine in this book. Throughout the Bible record, kings and kingdoms abound. The word for *king* in the Old Testament Scriptures is the word *melek,* which occurs there around 2,500 times.[30] One place the word appears is in Psalm 98, which was written as a "new song" of worship for God because "he has done marvelous things" (v. 1). After recounting the good things the Lord has done, the psalmist gives the imperative to "burst into jubilant song" (v. 4). Then in verse 6, the song cues the instruments: "With trumpets and the blast of the ram's horn – shout for joy before the LORD, the King." God's name in this verse is Ha Melek Jehovah. "The people of God respond with joyful singing to the accompaniment of musical instruments in celebration of Yahweh's universal kingship."[31] It is through Bible kings and kingdoms that we learn about our God as Ha Melek Jehovah.

The overwhelming majority of the kings in the Bible were wicked. Before Saul became king of Israel, the only ones who bore this title were leaders of the pagan nations that were opposed to the chosen people of God. However, after being led by Moses, Joshua, several prophets, and deliverers called judges, the people of Israel desired a king. Through the Spirit, Moses foresaw this day: "When you enter the land the LORD your God is giving you… and you say, 'Let us set a king over us like all the nations around us…'" (Deuteronomy 17:14).

This day eventually came about five hundred years later, at the end of the prophet Samuel's life, when the elders of Israel approached the old prophet and said, "You are old… Now appoint a king to lead us, such as all the other nations have" (I Samuel 8:5).

HA MELEK JEHOVAH'S RESPONSE

Samuel was devastated and disappointed by this request and shared his heartbreak with the Lord. God, however, was not surprised, telling his prophet to cooperate with the request: "Listen to all that the people are saying to you; it is not you they have rejected, but they have rejected me as their king" (v. 7). He went on to tell Samuel that they had been rejecting his leadership ever since he brought them out of Egypt. So the King the Lord did not force his sovereignty on his subjects. Instead, he gave the people over to their wishes for an earthly king, but this concession came with a warning. "Now listen to them; but warn them solemnly and let them know what the king who will reign over them will claim as his rights" (v. 9). In essence he was saying, OK, you want another king besides me? You're not going to like it, because and earthly king is not going to be like me, the only true King."

The prophet proceeded to tell the king-hungry Israelites what an earthly king would demand and exactly what this would cost them:

- A king will demand your families. "He will take your sons and make them serve with his chariots and horses" (v. 11). "Some he will assign to be commanders… others to plow his ground… others to make weapons of war" (v. 12).
- A king will demand your best. "He will take the best of your fields and vineyards and olive groves" (v. 14).

- A king will demand your money. "He will take a tenth of your flocks" (v. 17).
- A king will demand your service. "You yourselves will become his slaves" (v. 17).

Samuel tried to reason with the Israelites by raising questions in their minds. Did they really want to take God off the throne and replace him with a mere man? Were they really willing to transfer the crown to an imperfect being, one who was prone to pride, greed, and selfishness? Would they bow in homage to a finite creation instead of their infinite Creator? Samuel warned them that they would "cry out for relief" (v. 18).

"But the people refused to listen to Samuel. 'No!' they said. "We want a king over us" (v. 19). Their response sounds like one we might hear in our culture today.

FOUR REGAL QUESTIONS

While we may not live today under a literal monarchy, we have a heart's throne. And there we crown what is important and bow down to that as king. Rightfully, only God belongs on the throne of our lives. Only Ha Melek Jehovah will consistently rule our lives fairly, protect us absolutely, concern himself with our well-being, and act in our best interests. But like the Israelites, we often allow lesser kings to rule us, and we pay the price for putting someone (or something) else in God's place. If we take an introspective look at the warnings Samuel gave about earthly kings, we can probably determine who (or what) is the true ruler of our lives.

Readers of this book are not likely under the rule of a liberal, physical king. But a figurative king can hold sway over us; and that king makes the same royal demands named above: our families, our best, our money, and our service. Is there a king other than God on the throne of your heart? Consider these questions that correspond with Samuel's cautions.

Who makes the rules for your family?

Samuel said that a king would cost the people their families; they would have to do whatever the king ordered. In our culture today our jobs can demand too many of our hours – and rob our families of our needed presence. Our activities, hobbies, and interests don't plainly say, "You will not have time for your family if you pursue us." But such things can squander relationship opportunities with those we love, and they can "employ" family members in activities that should not necessarily have top priority.

- How many people miss church because of their children's sports tournaments week after week?
- How many families skip time together during dinner because their schedules don't align?
- How many families never pray or read the bible together, but *religiously* watch a weekly television show?

If the accepted cultural priorities of sports involvement, calendar over-commitment, or entertainment overload have invaded your home, it is likely these are ruling your family.

Who makes the rules for your best?

Pursuing graduation or a post-graduate degree takes hours of work, and many people deprive themselves of sleep, leisure activities, and close relationships in order to receive a diploma. Staying physically fit is healthy and can be a positive habit, but some become obsessed with working out – spending hours sweating and building muscle each day at the gym. Climbing the corporate ladder will require extra hours, attention to detail, and seeking the boss's approval through "above and beyond the call" work – but there can be a price to pay for all the extra effort.

The simple truth is that many of us give our best effort, our greatest passion, and our highest quality performance to things of this world that we deem to be important. Could it be that the energy we exert in these pursuits reveals what we truly worship?

Who makes the rules for your money?

One of the most revealing spiritual exercises you can do is to look at your monthly bank statement and see what you spend your money on. Jesus said, "Where your treasure is, there your heart will be also" (Matthew 6:21), and there is nothing that reveals our hearts more than this simple inventory. I have to confess that at times, based on this exercise, I have treasured my morning coffee more than contributing to the kids in my church who are raising money for a mission trip.

Alongside the actual frivolous spending comes submission to the societal expectation of overspending at Christmas, buying a bigger house to match your higher tax bracket, buying your sixteen-year-old a new car, or spending thousands of dollars on a wedding. A popular TV commercial asks, "What's in your wallet?" Could it be your king?

Who makes the rules for your service?

Nearly everyone voluntarily serves others in one form or another. Moms serve by doing the family's laundry. Adolescents serve as "book buddies" at school to help younger students learn how to read. Dads give hours of coaching the Little League team. Parents run the concession stands for the soccer club. Volunteers build houses for under-resourced families, serve food at homeless shelters, and pick up trash along the highways. Motivation for service may be varied, but it reveals each person's hierarchy of importance. All these acts of service are fine in and of themselves, but they can become obsession. Remember, Samuel said that a king would turn them into slaves – and there are thousands of organizations that would love to own *your* service. The question is whether you are serving because a movement, cause or mission owns you. Jesus challenges us: "No one can serve two masters" (Matthew 6:24).

A FAILED MONARCHY

In the way we prioritize the demands made on our families, our best, our money, and our service, we actually declare kingship in our lives. The Israelites had grown tired of bringing tithes to God the King. The Hebrew nation didn't want to worship him with burnt offerings anymore. Though their King had given them victory over their enemies, they didn't want to work to establish his kingdom. They had other goals. They wanted to be like the other nations. All the cool nations had kings, and now the Israelites wanted God to step aside as their own king and let someone else assume the throne.

We don't have to repeat their mistake. Whether we submit to the rules of Ha Melek Jehovah or not, he is absolutely King. Unlike earthly kings, he does not force his subjects to worship him; he invites them to. It's true that someday everyone – no longer able to deny that God *is* the one and only King – will bow before him, but his desire is for us to willingly submit to his kingship (see Hebrews 12:9; James 4:7). I think about all the times we place a variety of imperfect people, passions, and possessions on the throne of our respective hearts. How that must grieve the Lord! I can't help but hear the same tone of sadness in his voice that must have been there when he said to Samuel about Israel: "Listen to them and give them a king" (I Samuel 8:22).

> **All the cool nations had kings, and now the Israelites wanted God to step aside as their own King and let someone else assume the throne.**

Perhaps the series of kings who reigned over the Old Testament people of God was to serve as one huge object lesson, something God had planned that would illustrate his superiority over all kings. Even a casual historic glimpse reveals that the human kings of God's people were inferior. The wicked, selfish kings ruling God's people far outnumbered the righteous ones.

The history of this kingdom is bleak: Saul became king in 1050 BC. The kingdom divided in 930 BC. Assyria conquered the northern kingdom in 722; Babylon conquered the southern kingdom of Judah in 586. It all ended just as Samuel had warned. The people had wanted more, and these earthly kings brought more – but not in a good way. They brought:

- More pain than pleasure
- More oppression than freedom
- More defeat than victory
- More poverty than prosperity
- More paganism than true worship

In short, replacing God with human kings had been a disastrous failure. But God allowed human kingship because he had a plan for reestablishing his throne and his rightful place on it for eternity. The King and Lord would assume the throne through the lineage of a king named David.

THE COMING KING AND KINGDOM

"After the king was settled in his palace and the LORD had given him rest from all his enemies around him, he said to Nathan the prophet, 'Here I am, living in a house of cedar, while the ark of God remains in a tent'" (2 Samuel 7:1-2). Thus began the conversation between the earthly king after God's heart, David and the eternal King, Ha Melek Jehovah. "David decides that the time has finally come for him to do what any self-respecting king worthy of the name should do: build a house for his God."[32] David couldn't get past the fact that while he sat on an earthly throne in a palace, the Lord's throne (the Ark of the Covenant) was housed in a tent. David wanted to honor his King with a palace, and he asked Nathan the prophet to seek God's will concerning this endeavor. Nathan complied, and the word of the Lord came to him.

In the end, David was not the man God would choose to build his house; there was too much blood on his hands from all the wars he had fought. However, God's plan for reclaiming the throne of his people directly involved King David! There are two key verses that give great insight into this plan for kingship restored.

2 Samuel 7:12. "When your days are over and you rest with your ancestors, I will raise up your offspring to succeed you, your own flesh and blood, and I will establish his kingdom." The key word in this verse is the Hebrew word *zera,* translated as *offspring.* The word has to do with sowing, but also indicates the reproductive contribution of the man – and is often translated *seed.*[33] God was promising that someone related to David would always be on the throne, one who literally would come from his reproductive DNA. In the short term, this spoke of David's son Solomon, but in the long term it pointed to God's Son, Jesus!

Genesis 3:15. What is significant here is that this continued the string of "seed" promises that concerned the coming King/Messiah that began in Genesis 3:15. There God promised that Eve's seed would always conflict with Satan's seed… and eventually crush his head. It is the same word used to speak of Abraham's "descendants" in Genesis 17:7 and God's covenant with them. Now God was using the same word to speak of David's descendant and goes on to say: "I will establish the throne of his kingdom forever" (2 Samuel 7:12, 13).

In the New Testament the apostle Paul used the Greek equivalent of this word *seed (sperma)* to connect Jesus with Eve, Abraham, and David when he wrote, "Scripture does not say 'and to seeds,' meaning many people, but 'and to your seed,' meaning one person, who is Christ" (Galatians 3:16). "The trajectory from the Abrahamic covenant through the Davidic covenant to the new covenant in Christ is strengthened by the repetition of the words such as 'seed' used in the messianic sense."[34]

Jesus is the embodiment of the seed that would destroy Satan, perpetuate the family of Abraham, and sit as the rightful King on the eternal throne of King David. Ha Melek Jehovah became flesh and lived among us. Jesus crushed Satan's head by conquering death and the grave. He became the Abrahamic blessing of all nations by giving all people a way to God. Jesus became the rightful heir to the monarchy of his earthly forefather David by sitting on the throne of spiritual Israel (that is, the church worldwide) as Lord of all. Jesus was and is the King the Lord in human flesh, and he rules both now and forever – now, in the hearts of his people, and forever, over all.

The New Testament is clear that Jesus is the embodiment of God the King. For instance:

- Nathanael identified Jesus as "the king of Israel" because Jesus showed miraculous knowledge of his private conversation (John 1:49).
- Peter made the "good confession" of Jesus as Christ ("Messiah"); he understood that Jesus was the anointed king promised to Israel (Matthew 16:16).
- As Christ triumphantly entered Jerusalem on Passover Sunday before his crucifixion, the people shouted, "Blessed is the king who comes in the name of the Lord!" (Luke 19:38).
- The teachers of the law mockingly asked Jesus to prove he was the Messiah, the king of Israel, by miraculously coming down from the cross (Mark 15:32).
- Pilate asked Jesus if he were the king of the Jews (Matthew 27:11), then later posted that title on the cross on which he was crucified (Luke 23:38).

- When the people of Thessalonica accused the Christians in that city, they maintained that the Christians were teaching that there was "another king" besides Caesar, "one called Jesus" (Acts 17:7).
- In 1 Timothy 1:17 the apostle Paul practically broke into song about God, the "King eternal." Later he called God "the blessed and only ruler, the King of kings and Lord of lords" (6:15).
- At the end of time, Jesus (the Lamb) will overcome because he is "Lord of lords and King of kings" (Revelation 17:14).

The witness of the revelation paints an awesome picture of a victorious ruler with his kingly title written on his robe and thigh (19:16).

SUBMITTING TO HIS AUTHORITY

As the embodiment of Ha Melek Jehovah, Jesus is absolutely sovereign in the universe. Though the whole world is ultimately under his power, it is believers who recognize him as our Redeemer and Savior who loves us enough to lay his life down for us. We are subject to his greatness and power and, as such, are required to submit to his kingly authority. We *want* to submit to his kingly authority, and he does make royal demands of the citizens of his kingdom.

What demands does he make of us? And what advantage is there for us to serve King Jesus?

Let's return again to the template of demands offered by Samuel to see what our King requires of us – and to affirm why we would want no other King.

When Jesus rules your family

On the one hand, our King demands that our allegiance to him takes precedence over allegiance to our families. On the other, he has made his followers part of his royal family. In the New Testament Jesus spoke of a man who wanted to bury his father first and then come follow Jesus. Jesus challenged the man to "let the dead bury their own dead, but you go and proclaim the kingdom of God" (Luke 9:60). When speaking to a crowd that was following him, Jesus said, "If anyone comes to me and does not hate father and mother, wife and children, brothers and sisters – yes, even their own life – such a person cannot be my disciple" (14:26).

Jesus was not against families. In fact, he was subject to his earthly parents and quoted one of Moses' commandments to honor one's parents. He simply demands that our families take second place to him as King of our lives.

But unlike earthly kings, Jesus makes us part of his family by calling those who prioritize him above family brothers and sisters. "Pointing to his disciples, he said, 'Here are my mother and my brothers'" (Matthew 12:49). In his parable of the sheep and the goats, Jesus (as King on Judgment Day) said that the poor, hungry, naked, and imprisoned people of his day (the least of these) were part of his family. "The King will reply, 'Truly I tell you, whatever you did for one of the least of these brothers and sisters of mine, you did for me'" (25:40). Our King is royalty, but he welcomes us to be a part of his family, thereby making *us* royalty. "Both the one who makes people holy and those who are made holy are of the same family. So Jesus is not ashamed to call them brothers and sisters" (Hebrews 2:11).

The King of Israel would require people to do whatever he said. We need to do what King Jesus says. But when we allow this King to rule over our human family, we are not oppressed. Rather, we're invited into his superior heavenly family.

When Jesus rules your best

On the one hand, our King calls us to give our best as we live in his kingdom as obedient servants. On the other, he has given us his best: he finished the work to bring about our salvation. Every king who gives commands expects them to be obeyed; every king expects results. King Jesus spent much of his three-year ministry teaching and instructing, and he expected his followers to obey his words. Jesus stated, "Anyone who loves me will obey my teaching... Anyone who does not love me will not obey my teaching" (John 14:23, 24). Using the imagery of oxen lowing in the field, he said, "Take my yoke upon you and learn from me" (Matthew 11:29). He also recommended the kind of attitude his followers must have, when he said, "When you have done everything you were told to do, [you] should say, 'We are unworthy servants; we have only done our duty'" (Luke 17:10).

> **Everyone wants Jesus as Savior, but Jesus also expects to be in charge. He is both Savior and *LORD*!**

Make no mistake about it – Jesus expects our best; he demands our obedience to his ways. When I lead our new-member class at church, I often remind people to listen carefully to the confession we take before baptizing someone. Everyone wants Jesus as Savior, but Jesus also expects to be in charge. He is both Savior and *Lord*! At the same time, Jesus has completed the work on our behalf that only he could accomplish. He did this by becoming obedient, by giving his best for our best.

- "He humbled himself by becoming obedient to death – even death on a cross!" (Philippians 2:8).
- "I lay down my life – only to take it up again. No one takes it from me, but I lay it down of my own accord. I have authority to lay it down and authority to take it up again" (John 10:17, 18).
- As the time drew close for him to die, Jesus prayed about the work he was about to do. "Now my soul is troubled, and

what shall I say? 'Father, save me from this hour'? No, it was for this very reason I came to this hour" (12:27).

• Finally, Jesus noted that his work on our behalf was complete, when he said, "It is finished" (19:30).

Our King asks us to obey, but by *his* obedience to death on a cross he worked out our salvation.

When Jesus rules your money

On the one hand, our King demands that we give him all of everything we own. On the other, he has redeemed us from the clutches of death and paid the very high price for our sin.

When I preach on stewardship, I often joke with my congregation that the twenty-first-century American loophole concerning giving is that tithing is not commanded in the New Testament. My response? "That's true. Let's ignore the Old Testament pattern of giving a tenth and just go with Jesus' standard instead." I remind them that Jesus said, "Those of you who do not give up everything you have cannot be my disciples" (Luke 14:33). Then I add, "With this new understanding on giving, I'm expecting a great offering today!"

The truth is that every offering we take is only a small fraction of what God has given us, and we can never repay him. Everything we have already belongs to him anyway.

Samuel told the Israelites that a king would take a tenth of their wealth. And while Jesus demands more – our all – he is aware of a debt we can never pay. Our King was very much aware that our sins carried a death sentence with them (Romans 6:23). When he spoke to the unbelieving Jews, he said, "I told you that you would die in your sins; if you do not believe that I am he, you will indeed die in your sins" (John 8:24). He was completely aware that no one could claim to be without sin. As he said to the accusers of the adulteress, "Let any one of you who is without sin be the first to throw a stone at her" (v. 7).

So he did what no earthly king has ever done for those subject to him. Jesus willingly sacrificed his life so that our penalty for sin would not result in death. On the night he was betrayed, he spoke of his atoning work on our behalf through his death: "This is my blood of the covenant, which is poured out for many for the forgiveness of sins" (Matthew 26:28). He gave his life as the ultimate way of paying our way. "For even the Son of Man did not come to be served, but to serve, and to give his life as a ransom for many" (Mark 10:45). And he gave his life – his all – as a sign of his friendship with us. "Greater love has no one than this: to lay down one's life for one's friends" (John 15:13).

Through Jesus' willful giving, God the King paid the price for our sins when we could not.

When Jesus rules your service

On the one hand, our King demands our very lives in his service. On the other, he has given his life so that we could live full lives now and forever. Jesus will not tolerate anything less than our all. He once said to the crowds who followed him, "Whoever wants to be my disciple must deny themselves and take up their cross daily and follow me" (Luke 9:23). In fact, our King teaches that any effort to keep one's life will disqualify that person from the kingdom. "Whoever tries to keep their life will lose it, and whoever loses their life will preserve it" (17:33).

Our King, Ha Melek Jehovah, came to earth to give his life for us. In a kingly conversation, the governor Pilate asked Jesus if he was the king of the Jews; and Jesus replied, "You have said so" (Matthew 27:11). Later when they talked, Jesus explained why he was willing to die even though he was the King. "My kingdom is not of this world. If it were, my servants would fight to prevent my arrest by the Jewish leaders. But now my kingdom is from another place" (John 18:36).

When Jesus died, he was at his kingly best. A crown of thorns adorned his head, the blood of redemption ran down, and the sign above him said "JESUS OF NAZARETH, THE KING OF THE JEWS" (19:19). Our King died for us!

Samuel warned the Israelites that they would resent being "slaves" to their king and would "cry out for relief." How different it is to be in the service of our King!

O WORSHIP THE *RIGHT* KING!

When I was about ten years old, my father (who was a fast-pitch softball enthusiast) took me to a spectacular demonstration of perhaps the greatest softball pitcher ever to play the game. Throughout the 1970's, Eddie Feigner toured around the country with four other players as the self-proclaimed King and His Court. He was really good! I watched in amazement as he struck out batters while blindfolded. He struck out batters though pitching from behind his back, between his legs, and even standing at second base! On the softball diamond, he certainly was king. But an athletic field is a very small kingdom.

In my lifetime, Elvis has been called the King of Rock 'n' Roll, and Michael Jackson was given the title of King of Pop... in the small kingdom of the music industry. LeBron James, nicknamed King James, has been a phenom in the sport of basketball since he was in high school, and in 2012 he was crowned champion more than once.

I have come into contact with some of those kinds of kings and their kingdoms. And I have read about the kings of biblical history. All of them have come to an end – or will someday. But there is one kingdom that is established forever, and its King is eternal. Ha Melek Jehovah is the name of that King. Why would we want any other?

FIRST-NAME BASIS
For individual or group study

1. Have you ever come into contact with royalty? If so, what happened? What emotions did you feel when you had your brush with fame?
2. Of all the kings (or queens) in history, which one would you most like to meet and why?
3. In your opinion, what is the major problem with giving absolute authority to a human being? What is it about being a king that can take a good person and corrupt him?
4. What trait do you admire most about our God the King? Why?
5. Which of the four kingly demands mentioned in this chapter (your family, your best, your money, your service) are you most likely to allow onto the throne of your heart? What is the reason for naming the one you did? Which of the four presents the least threat for detracting from God's sovereignty in your life? Why?

GETTING ACQUAINTED WITH
HA MELEK JEHOVAH

1. Spend some time writing down what you would consider to be good traits of a perfect king. Why do you think these traits are important? Beside each item write down the way(s) in which God fulfills each characteristic as the perfect King.
2. People who wish they were in charge sometimes use the expression "If I were king for a day, I'd…" If you had absolute power and authority, and were king for a day, what would you do? Write an official proclamation announcing the realities of your kingdom. Then consider… What would Jesus change if he were to overthrow your kingdom? Spend some time listing the changes next to your edicts. Then use this as a daily prayer guide to declare Jesus as King of your life.

3. Kneeling is the most common display of submission before royalty. Spend time kneeling before God the King, worshipping him for allowing you to be his servant. While on your knees, bow your head and praise him for as many of his attributes (expressed through the names we have studied) as you can recall. You may want to use this sentence as a guide: "I worship you, O King, for you are _____."

NOTES

Endnotes

Introduction:

[1]http://www.blueletterbible.org/lang/lexicon/lexicon.
cfm?Strongs=H1961&t=KJV.

Chapter 1

Epigraph. J. I. Packer, *Knowing God* (Downers Grove, IL; InterVarsity Press, 1973 edition), 75.

[2]http://www.hebrew-streams.org/works/monotheism/context-elohim.html.

[3]http://quizlet.com/5372770/genesis-clarkes-commentary-flash-cards.

[4]Bruce K. Waltke, *Genesis: A Commentary* (Grand Rapids, MI: Zondervan, 2001), 58

[5]R. Kent Hughes, *Genesis: Beginning and Blessing* (Wheaton, IL: Crossway Books, 2004), 20.

[6]www.blueletterbible.org/lang/lexicon/lexicon.
cmf?Strongs=H6213&t=KJV.

[7]C. F. Keil and F. Delitzsch, *Commentary on the Old Testament: The Pentateuch*, Volume 1 (Peabody, MA: Hendrickson Publishers, 2001), 30.

[8]Gordon J. Wenham, *Word Biblical Commentary*, Volume 1 (Waco, TX: Word Books, 1987), 60-61 and www.blueletterbible.org notes on Genesis 2:7; Job 34:14.

[9]Hughes, 52.

Chapter 2

Epigraph. Corrie Ten Boom, www.dailychristianquote.com.

[10]Since scholars have not come to a clear consensus on the ages of Abraham and Isaac at the time of this test, I have used the Scriptures referring to Abraham and Ishamel's ages to estimate the age of each here. Abraham was 99 years old when God renewed his promise through the covenant of circumcision (Genesis 17:1), Isaac would be born a year later (v. 21), and Ishmael was thirteen (v. 25). While I've settled on age fifteen for Isaac here, some sources put Isaac as old as thirty-seven. One considered him to be thirty-three (which would, if true, make an interesting parallel to Jesus' age at the time he became the sacrifice Lamb).

[11]Keil and Delitzsch, 598.

[12]*The Expositor's Bible Commentary*, Volume 2. Frank E. Gaebelein, general editor (Grand Rapids, MI: Zondervan, 1990), 169.

[13]Hughes, 303.

Chapter 3

Epigraph. Philip Yancey, *Reaching for the Invisible God* (Grand Rapids, MI: Zondervan, 2000), 76.

[14]*The Names of God Bible,* Ann Spangler, general editor (Grand Rapids, MI: Revell/Baker Publishing Group, 2011), 100.

[15]Keith Blayney, "The Caduceus vs the Staff of Asclepius (Asklepian)," October 2005, www.drblayney, com/Asclepius.html.

[16]http://wwwstudylight.org/lex/grk/view.cgi?number=4982.

[17]I. Howard Marshall, *Luke: Historian & Theologian* (Downers Grove, IL: InterVarsity Press, third edition 1988), 95.

Chapter 4

Epigraph, Howard Thurman, *Deep is the Hunger* (Richmond, IN: Friends United Press, 1990 reprint), 147.

Chapter 5

Epigraph. A. W. Tozer, compiled by Anita M. Bailey, *That Incredible Christian* (Camp Hill, PA: Christian Publications, 1964 edition), 27.

[18]www.usmarshals.gov/witsec/index.html.

[19]www.blueletterbible.org/lang/lexicon/lexicon.cmf?Strongs=H6635&t=NIV

[20]www.bible.org/article/book-Psalms#P133-19917.

Chapter 6

Epigraph. Joseph M. Stowell, *The Dawn's Early Light* (Chicago: Moody Press, 1990), 57.

[21]C. F Keil and F. Delitzsch, *Commentary on the Old Testament: Psalms,* Volume 5 (Peabody, MA: Hendrickson Publishers, 2001), 226.

[22]http://blueletterbible.org/lang/lexicon/lexicon. cfm?strongs=G5461&t=NIV and http://www.preceptaustin. org/2corinthians_43-4_commentary.htm.

Chapter 7

Epigraph. Jerry Bridges, *Transforming Grace: Living Confidently in God's Unfailing Love* (Colorado Springs, CO: NavPress, 1991), 19.

[23]www.blueletterbible.org/lang/lexicon/lexicon. cmf?strongs=H4190&t=NIV.

[24]*The Expositor's Bible Commentary,* Volume 5, Frank E. Gaebelein, general editor (Grand Rapids, MI: Zondervan, 1991), 450.

[25]www.blueletterbible.org/lang/lexicon/lexicon. cmf?strongs=H3467&t=NIV.

[26]*Zondervan NIV Study Bible,* Kenneth L. Barker, general editor (Grand Rapids, MI: Zondervan, 2002 revision), 390.

[27]*The Expositor's Bible Commentary,* Volume 3, Frank E. Gaebelein, general editor (Grand Rapids, MI: Zondervan, 1992), 636.

[28]Ibid.

Chapter 8

Epigraph. Gene Edwards, *A Tale of Three Kings* (Wheaton, IL: Tyndale House Publishers, 1992), 78.

[29] Suzanne Swan, main contributor, *Eyewitness Travel Guides: Turkey* (Cape Town, South Africa: Struik New Holland Publishing, 2006 edition), 68.

[30] www.blueletterbible.org/lang/lexicon/lexicon. cmf?Strongs=H4428&t=KJV&page=58.

[31] *The Expositor's Bible Commentary,* Volume 5, 629.

[32] *The Expositor's Bible Commentary,* Volume 3, 884.

[33] www.blueletterbible.org/lang/lexicon/lexicon. cmf?Strongs=H2233&t=NIV.

[34] *The Expositor's Bible Commentary,* Volume 3, 890.

Printed in the United States
By Bookmasters